LAKELAND
50TH ANNIVERSARY
Recipe Book

We know our customers love to cook and to celebrate our 50th birthday, we asked you to send us your most special recipes. A huge thank you to everybody who sent them in – as you can imagine it was really difficult to choose, but we finally got there and here they are! Lakeland would also like to thank the chefs and celebrities who shared their recipes for our anniversary book. Children in Need is a charity close to our hearts and we are delighted to donate the proceeds from our book to this worthy charity.

RMC Books would like to thank Steven Doherty of the First Floor Café (www.firstfloorcafe.co.uk) and Fancie (www.fancie.co.uk) for their help with testing and preparing recipes for photography.

All proceeds from each book sold will benefit BBC Children in Need (charity number 802052 in England & Wales and SC039557 in Scotland)

Lakeland 50th Anniversary Recipe Book

CONTENTS

50 YEARS OF CREATIVE HOME AND KITCHENWARE by LAKELAND

THE LAKELAND STORY
By Sam Rayner

Fifty years ago, three brothers in need of pocket money during the school holidays started counting polythene bags in their garage to help their dad out. Those lads were me, Sam Rayner, and my brothers Martin and Julian. At the time we had no idea where this endeavour would take us but, by sticking to our father Alan's philosophy of 'always look after the customer and the business will look after itself', we've built Lakeland into one of the most successful kitchenware companies in the UK.

LAKELAND PLASTICS (Windermere) LTD.

(Incorporating Lakeland Poultry Packers)

High Street, WINDERMERE, Westmorland.

Tel. WINDERMERE 969

1960s
Plastic fantastic

Lakeland Plastics

1970s
The big freeze

1980s
Microwave madness

LAKELAND *Plastics*

THE CREATIVE KITCHENWARE COMPANY

1990s
Heading for the high street

LAKELAND LIMITED

2000s
Web mania

2010s
Spreading our wings

1960s

Taking the
SHOW ON THE ROAD

Our story began with those bags we used to count. While selling animal feed from farm to farm, Dad bought chickens to sell at Kendal market – Thursday was pluck and prep day at our house. Presented in plastic bags, our dressed birds stole the show, outselling the other smallholders. As more and more farmers began to freeze poultry, they needed plastic bags and Dad knew just where to find them. Word spread quickly and, as demand for his bags took off, Lakeland Poultry Packers was formed with Dad regularly driving his Morris 1000 van to the factory near London to pick up supplies.

Back in Windermere, we counted the bags into packs of 100 ready for sale. In the early days, our mum Dorothy used to run the mail order despatch from home, hence my brothers and I regularly found ourselves perching precariously on boxes of plastic bags as we watched television or read a book.

When we moved house in 1964, Mum and Dad continued to run a successful hotel business while operating their mail-order business from the garage. To help spread the word, they advertised in Farmers Weekly, Exchange and Mart, even The Lady Magazine, and soon found themselves supplying freezer bags and accessories to customers all over the country. Lakeland Plastics was born.

We also supplied haystack covers, silage sheeting and, of course, the innovative 'Lammacs' – plastic coats designed to protect newborn lambs from the elements. The 'plastics' went much further than simply polythene products – we sold freezers, egg boxes and even gourmet frozen foods too.

Alexandra Buildings Station Precinct
Windermere Cumbria
Telephone Windermere 2255

Alan Rayner

Dorothy Rayner

Direct mail suppliers to Agriculture, Industry and the Domestic Market

ALEXANDRA ROAD, WINDERMERE, Westmorland

Tel. Windermere 2255—Day and night service
(Messages recorded out of office hours by our ANSAFONE machine)

Our old warehouse on Alexandra Road

LAKELAND PLASTICS (Windermere) LTD.

(Incorporating Lakeland Poultry Packers)

High Street, WINDERMERE, Westmorland.

Tel. WINDERMERE 969

PLASTIC BAGS AND SHEETING

PRICE LIST

120 GAUGE POLYTHENE BAGS
Width first dimension

Size	10	100	500	1000
5" x 7"	—	3/-	13/6	24/-
7" x 9"	6d.	4/3	19/3	34/-
8" x 12"	8d.	5/6	25/-	44/-
11" x 16"	1/1	10/-	45/-	80/-
12" x 18"	1/4	11/6	51/6	93/-
16" x 20"	2/-	16/8	83/4	150/-
21" x 25"	3/-	25/-	125/-	225/-
Bag Ties	—	8d.	3/-	5/6
Colour Printed Bag 11" x 16"	1/6	14/-	63/-	112/-

150 GAUGE POLYTHENE BAGS

5" x 7"	—	3/6	16/-	28/-
8" x 12"	9d.	7/-	31/6	56/-
11" x 16"	1/4	12/6	56/-	100/-

ADHESIVE LABELS FOR BAGS

¾" Round	7d. per sheet of 40
1½" x 2"	6d. per sheet of 16

CLEAR POLYTHENE SHEETING
By the yard

Width	Standard	Heavy
24"	3d.	11d.
36"	4d.	1/6
48"	7½d.	2/-
72"	11d.	3/-
144"	1/10	6/-

BLACK POLYTHENE SHEETING

By the yard		Per 10' minimum	
	Standard		Medium
24"	4½d.	240"	10/6
36"	5d.	288"	12/6
48"	7d.		

SPECIAL BARGAIN
BALL POINT PENS—Guaranteed
6d. each   6 for 2/6

DESPATCH BY RETURN
Cash with Order—C.O.D. extra
Postage up to 10/-—1/6
,,   over 10/-—2/-
£2 and over Post Free

After a resounding success at the Royal Bath and West Show, the first agricultural show I recall, Dad began visiting shows around the country. Demand constantly outstripped supply – Martin even remembers having to drive overnight to replenish stock for the first five years we attended the Great Yorkshire Show. Eventually, we were taking four trailers to all the major shows around the country (our record was 120 between Easter and September!). As well as selling our wares, the shows became an ideal opportunity to build up our mailing list.

In the early days the entire family used to go 'on tour' and, with her good friends Kath and Beryl, our mum Dorothy would always have a hot meal ready for the whole team at the end of a long day. As we brothers got older, we used to spend summer driving our mobile exhibition units from as far north as Inverness to the most rural corners of Cornwall. Life on the road was hard work, but always eventful – from having to be winched off a humpback bridge to being stopped by flashing blue lights as the policeman driving the car wanted a catalogue for his wife! There are so many tales we could tell.

As our own families grew, they began to join us and I remember my wife Judy causing considerable alarm at the bank after one show when the cashiers discovered that her pram contained more than our firstborn. Peeling back the covers, she revealed the entire takings in cash – needless to say the manager was immediately summoned and the money transferred to a more secure location.

With all this diversification going on, Dad's garage was never going to be big enough so an old warehouse in Alexandra Road in Windermere was pressed into service as a parcel-packing area and small shop.

"Life on the road was hard work, but always eventful – from having to be winched off a humpback bridge to being stopped by flashing blue lights as the policeman driving the car wanted a catalogue for his wife!"

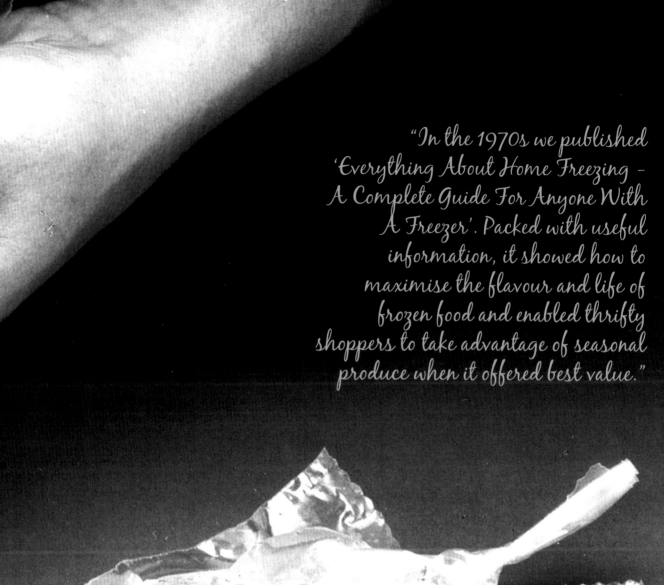

"In the 1970s we published 'Everything About Home Freezing – A Complete Guide For Anyone With A Freezer'. Packed with useful information, it showed how to maximise the flavour and life of frozen food and enabled thrifty shoppers to take advantage of seasonal produce when it offered best value."

1970s

The BIG FREEZE

Home freezing became the 'new big thing' and we quickly took it to heart. As well as selling to the general public, we began selling our 'Freezeasy' pack – a complete 'starter' pack for new freezer owners – to the electricity board and shops like Bejam and Electrolux. We wanted to show that batch freezing could be simple with the right equipment, and as testament to their longevity, many of those original essentials are still in the Lakeland range today.

We also published 'Everything About Home Freezing – A Complete Guide For Anyone With A Freezer'. Packed with useful information on growing, freezing and storing, it showed how to maximise the flavour and life of frozen food and, of course, enabled thrifty shoppers to take advantage of seasonal produce when it offered best value – very important to the household budget.

SHARE OUR ADVICE WITH YOUR CLUB OR FRIENDS

Our Home Freezing Advisory Service has a 20 minute film on home freezer packaging you can show free of charge! Since it was introduced in 1972, "Freezeasy" has been enjoyed by over 10,000 through clubs or with groups of friends. The film features Jess Mitchell and covers all aspects of freezer packaging showing the importance of using the right materials.

You can arrange a showing of this 16mm film by writing to Anne Slater. Send 75p (including post and packing and 25p deposit) The deposit will be returned if the film is sent back the day following your show. Give your anticipated date, an alternative, and the number of people expected to attend.

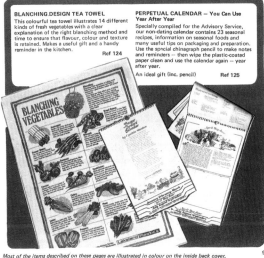

BLANCHING DESIGN TEA TOWEL
This colourful tea towel illustrates 14 different kinds of fresh vegetables with a clear explanation of the right blanching method and time to ensure that flavour, colour and texture is retained. Makes a useful gift and a handy reminder in the kitchen.
Ref 124

PERPETUAL CALENDAR — You Can Use Year After Year
Specially compiled for the Advisory Service, our non-dating calendar contains 23 seasonal recipes, information on seasonal foods and many useful tips on packaging and preparation. Use the special chinagraph pencil to make notes and reminders — then wipe the plastic-coated paper clean and use the calendar again — year after year.
An ideal gift (inc. pencil)   Ref 125

Most of the items described on these pages are illustrated in colour on the inside back cover.   9

The old station master's house which became our first real offices

The Rayner brothers — then

On the home front, Dad retired in 1974 and, returning from voluntary service in Uganda aged 21, I took over the running of the business alongside Martin, 23, and Julian, who was 16 and still at school.

Lakeland was leading the way when it came to home-freezing but the work was seasonal and, in a moment of inspiration, we got a glimpse of what must seem blindingly obvious to anyone now – people who froze food also cooked it! So along came the 'Everything For Home Cooking' catalogue. Our first one was very basic indeed, filled with black and white sketches of each product and printed by us.

Soon the demand for cooking equipment outweighed anything else and we scaled down the agricultural side to concentrate on all things kitchenware. The first items we sold were ground-based pans from Lune Metal Spinning and I remember loading the show unit with pans from their Morecambe factory – eventually we built an extension on the trailer which was known as 'Sam's Pan Stand'!

It was time once more to move to a bigger location and, when the disused Windermere station and yard came up for rent, we were able to set up our first real offices in the station master's house. The company was managed from the bedroom, orders were taken in the front room and the bathroom used to store customer records, piled up in the cast iron bath. The once-defunct station was buzzing again, with our products stored in the aptly named goods yard.

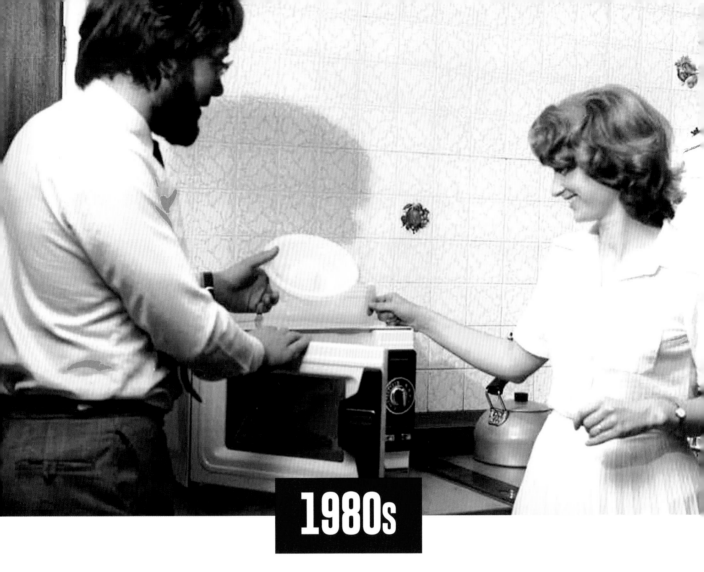

1980s

Mail order
PIONEERS

As we entered the 1980s, we progressed from a six-page leaflet to more substantial catalogues, widening our audience considerably. We couldn't afford photography in the early days but that didn't seem to matter – we were offering products customers wanted and couldn't buy anywhere else. But the time came when we realised we had to take that next step and have our catalogues produced in full colour – it was like changing the TV from black and white to colour! We even entered the technological age, inheriting our first computer which we used to store customer records.

Around this time, the new and mysterious microwave entered the market – just the sort of innovation we loved. So we set out to find the best microwave cookware on the market and, because our customers had lots of questions, set up Lakeland's Microwave Advisory Service too.

Still growing, we secured a sizeable piece of land next to our premises at the railway station in Windermere and at last were able to have a purpose-built facility with everyone under one roof and a flagship store to be proud of. This was a great leap forward and enabled us to become established as the leading supplier of innovative kitchen and homeware, gaining a reputation for excellent customer service.

Our first venture into the high street was in Chester – a tiny little shop in Eastgate Row. Julian and I fitted out the store along with some help from others. We didn't run to overnight accommodation then, so we slept in sleeping bags on the top floor. The reward for a hard day's work was to go to the Italian restaurant in the evening.

"As we entered the 1980s, we progressed to more substantial catalogues. We realised we had to take that next step and have them produced in full colour – it was like changing the TV from black and white to colour!"

LAKELAND *L* LIMITED

1990s

What's in A NAME?

The mid-nineties saw us move into home storage solutions and, by the end of the decade, our cleaning range was well established. As our range diversified, the name 'Lakeland Plastics' didn't sit well any more so, after much deliberation and many a sleepless night, we made the bold decision to drop the 'Plastics' and rename ourselves 'Lakeland Limited'. It was a huge gamble but we were soon reassured by a flood of comments such as 'about time too!' and haven't looked back since.

As we were rapidly outgrowing our premises in Windermere, we built a new distribution centre on land we'd had the foresight to purchase just up the road in Kendal. This building became the heart of the business and the base for replenishing shelves in our Windermere mail order despatch department and in our growing number of stores.

This was the decade when our retail business really took off, with stores popping up on high streets up and down the country – from historical buildings like the Ancient House in Ipswich, which still houses a museum, to Bluewater, one of the largest shopping centres in the UK.

As the millennium approached, we joined the world wide web. While all around us businesses were worrying about the 'millennium bug', we took our first steps towards our website, initially so customers could join our mailing list, but today it has become a large part of our business.

The Ipswich store

The Bluewater store

The First Floor Café

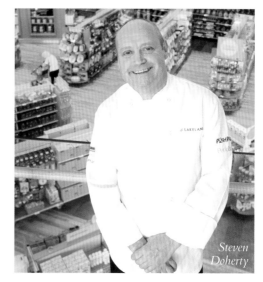

Steven Doherty

Our Customer Director Michelle Kershaw

2000s

Bigger & BETTER

As we entered the millennium it became clear we were running out of space in Windermere. The solution was to extend our Kendal distribution site so parcel-packing could be relocated, allowing us to send out thousands of orders every day – a far cry from the days when my brothers and I used to wheel parcels to the post office on a trolley! The space created at Windermere was transformed into our modern flagship store, more than double the size of our old shop and one of the most popular visitor attractions in the Lakes.

Our new store deserved a smart new café and we were lucky to be joined by Steven Doherty and his wife Marj. In 1985 Steven became the first ever Brit to be head chef of a three-Michelin-star establishment and for the next five years Le Gavroche won every major European food accolade and maintained its three-star status. Together Steven and Marj have turned the First Floor Café into a real dining must. Steven's spent hours in the kitchen recreating the recipes we received for this book and I can tell you there are some real crackers!

In May 2004, our much-loved Customer Director Michelle Kershaw sadly passed away after over 35 years of being the 'face of Lakeland'. An expert on all things microwave and freezer, many of our customers told us they felt like they'd lost a friend too. It soon became obvious that customers missed having one person here in Windermere to represent their views, so Wendy Miranda became our Customer Ambassador, and was coaxed away from the Tunbridge Wells store where she'd been manager for over a decade. Now the eyes, ears and voice of our customers, she ensures we keep up the service that sets us apart from the rest. Later in the decade, Lakeland Plastics, or plain old Lakeland to loyal 'Lakelanders', became known simply as Lakeland.

2010s

Here's to a
BRIGHT FUTURE

Our small 'family' has certainly flourished and now numbers just under 1800 colleagues. Team spirit is implicit in our philosophy so we only employ people who embrace our values of honesty, trust and innovation. Placing a huge emphasis on training, we look after our team and in return we know they will look after you, our customers.

Many colleagues have been with us for 10, 15 or 20 years… and a few for a remarkable 30 or even 40! Julian was still at school when he signed Malcolm's work experience contract, and after 40 years' service, when Malcolm's not helping out at our stores or shows you'll find him in our Windermere store. Another young lad, Mark, used to be picked up after school for the weekend show run in the seventies and these days you will find him in our Buying Department. Wherever you turn you'll find mums, dads, sons and daughters, sisters and brothers all working together as part of our team – in some cases, three generations of one family! We all know each other by first name and Lakeland really is a warm and friendly place to work. It's true what they say: 'happy staff create happy customers!'

We're approaching 70 stores up and down the country. We opened in Northern Ireland for the first time during this decade, and are constantly looking to open more. In 2010 we opened our very first overseas store in Dubai where Lakeland has been warmly embraced and we now have stores in over seven countries. Believe it or not, the best sellers in the Middle East are the same as in the UK – people all over the world love to cook and bake, and enjoy sharing their creations with family and loved ones.

Catalogues got the high-tech treatment too – virtual catalogues and our award-winning magazine app mean customers can browse digitally, wherever they are. We also launched our Facebook page so we can keep in touch with the online Lakeland community – we love to see and hear how our products help in the kitchen and all around the home.

Although mail order is still going strong, we've seen a shift towards internet shopping with more people than ever choosing to order online. Our comprehensive website is over 10 years old and we're constantly improving it so it's friendlier and easier to use than ever. We've also branched out into Europe, launching our German website a year ago – it's going from strength to strength, bringing the Lakeland range to a whole new audience. And we recently launched a Middle East website to support our stores in that region.

Here at Lakeland we embrace change but some things remain constant. Top of that list are our customers and our colleagues. We're constantly asked what the secret to our success is and it really is quite simple: you need to look after your customers. Ever since we started all those years ago, we've insisted our customers receive two things – the highest quality paired with value for money.

Customers are still the heart of our business and we know how important it is to listen to what they have to say – they're the reason we're here! We receive hundreds of letters and emails every day asking for advice, letting us know how we're doing and, of course, suggesting products to sell. One such suggestion came from Patricia Laycock from Frome in Somerset who wished to bake Pudsey Bear cookies to sell for charity and wanted us to make a Pudsey Bear cookie cutter... the rest, as they say, is history! To date we have sold over 300,000 cutters in various guises and with your help we've donated over £1million to Children in Need. Our fundraising efforts for this very worthwhile charity continue and that's why all the profits from this 50th Anniversary Recipe Book will also be going straight to Children in Need.

Sam with staff at the Dubai store

It's been an absolute pleasure to share the Lakeland journey with you – I hope you enjoyed the trip too. Thank you for your loyal custom, and here's to the next 50 years!

✐LAKELAND
Cooking all over the world!

"People all over the world love to cook and bake, and enjoy sharing their creations with family and loved ones."

"We are constantly asked what the key to our success is and it really is quite simple... take care of your customers and the business will take care of itself."

STARTERS

Angela Corbett
STUFFED MUSHROOMS WITH GARLIC & CHEESE

///

This is a favourite with my friends who are vegetarian or who prefer a change from meat dishes.

SERVES 8

8 large mushrooms
200g grated Cheddar
20g grated Parmigiano Reggiano or
Parmesan, for the topping
2 tbsp rapeseed oil
1 bunch spring onions, finely chopped
4 asparagus tips, finely chopped
4 tbsp fresh breadcrumbs
½ tsp garlic salt or granules
2 tbsp fresh flat parsley, finely chopped or
2 tsp dried parsley
Pepper, to season

I prefer the Parmigiano Reggiano for the topping as it is nutty, but if you cannot get it use grated Parmesan.

METHOD

Preheat grill to a medium temperature.

Take the stalk from the centre of the mushrooms. Finely chop to add to the mixture. Brush the mushrooms with the oil, place on a tray cap side upwards and grill for five minutes.

Prepare the mixture for the filling. Place into a bowl all the ingredients except the cheese for the topping and the pepper and mix thoroughly. When mixed, season with the pepper.

Bring the mushrooms from under the grill, turn each one over and fill with the mixture, then on the top sprinkle the grated Parmigiano Reggiano or Parmesan.

Place back under the grill until there is a golden brown crust on top of the filling mix.

Serve with salad and crusty bread if desired.

★ *These ingredients are for eight starters or four lunch mains.*

Angela Corbett, Bedfordshire
"I have always loved cooking and entertaining. I am the cook at the Shillington Congregational Church, which I have attended all my life. I found that I needed to do something different for vegetarians and this recipe is one which the people like. I have been a Lakeland customer for over 30 years. Lakeland products are always first class and good value."

Anne Till
PANEER STUFFED AUBERGINES

//

SERVES 4

4 large aubergines
400g paneer cheese, patted dry and cut
into 1cm cubes
700g ripe tomatoes, diced
200g baby plum tomatoes, halved
2 onions, finely diced
2 tbsp Madras curry paste (more if you
like it spicier)
1 tsp kalonji seeds
Salt and pepper, to season
Oil, for cooking

METHOD

Preheat the oven to 180°C.

Halve the aubergines lengthways. Score the flesh, taking care not to cut through the skin. Place cut-side up on a baking tray. Spray with a little oil and season well.

Bake for 45-55 minutes until soft. Cool for a few minutes so they are cool enough to handle. Scoop out the flesh, again taking care not to break the skin.

Place the empty shells on the baking tray and set aside.

Roughly chop the flesh and place in a mixing bowl.

Fry the onions in oil until beginning to soften. Stir in the curry paste and cook for 2-3 minutes until fragrant. Tip in the chopped tomatoes. Cook until they become pulpy and a bit saucy. Scrape into the mixing bowl. Add in the plum tomatoes and paneer cheese. Season and add the kalonji seeds. Stir together.

Spoon into the empty aubergine shells.

Bake for 25-35 minutes until piping hot and beginning to colour.

Serve on a bed of baby spinach with chutneys and naan breads.

Anne Till, Stafford
"I have been a Lakeland customer for more years than I can remember. My first item was a health grill for my 15th birthday from my mum and dad. I remember being really excited about it and pestering my parents for it for ages after seeing it in the catalogue. I entered the competition because I love to cook and one of my passions is to create recipes which get tested on friends and family. I fill notebooks with my recipe ideas and have long dreamed of writing my own cookbook."

Carole Christofis
GOATS' CHEESE & ROASTED VEGETABLE LOG

//

SERVES 8-10

250g spreadable goats' cheese
500g vegetables of choice – suggest
courgettes, mushrooms, carrots, baby
tomatoes, peppers, aubergine
500g block of ready-roll puff pastry, rolled
approx. 30x20cm
1 beaten egg

METHOD

Slice the vegetables (leave baby tomatoes whole) and place in an oven at 180-200°C for 20-30 minutes.

Remove the vegetables from oven and leave until cool.

Slice the goats' cheese into half-centimetre rounds.

Roll the puff pastry thinly and place on a baking tray.

Arrange the cooked mixed vegetables along one side of the pastry.

Place the sliced goats' cheese on top of the vegetables.

Fold over the puff pastry and secure the edges.

Insert a fork into top of puff pastry a couple of times to allow steam to escape.

Brush the top of the pastry with the beaten egg.

Cook for approximately one hour at 200°C until sufficiently browned.

Enjoy with mixed salad and tiny roasted potato cubes cooked with garlic.

Carole Christofis is a Lakeland customer from Hertfordshire.

Caroline Brookes
SCALLOP GRATIN

//

SERVES 4

12 medium scallops
100g spinach
25g butter
25g plain flour
285ml milk
Splash of dry white wine
75g grated mature Cheddar
½ leek, finely sliced
2 tbsp breadcrumbs
Salt and white pepper, to season

Caroline Brookes, London
"I often bake for my work colleagues and sometimes hold cake sales to raise funds, or just bake them something as a treat! Often with celebration meals, the recipes can be complicated, with several stages and a huge list of ingredients. I feel this recipe is relatively simple, and I wanted to show that you can make tasty, affordable and elegant looking food, without spending hours in the kitchen. With so many well known retailers disappearing from the high street, 50 years is a real achievement. It's good to know that the Lakeland brand will continue to grow."

METHOD

Preheat the oven to 200°C.

Sauté the spinach in a frying pan for a couple of minutes until softened. Squeeze any excess moisture from the spinach, remove and leave to one side.

In the same pan, melt the butter and stir in the flour, cooking on a low heat for a couple of minutes.

Gradually add the milk to the flour and butter, stirring continuously until you have a smooth sauce.

Stir in 50g of the cheese and a splash of dry white wine, along with seasoning to taste.

Add the leeks to the sauce and simmer for a couple of minutes.

Take the sauce off the heat and add the scallops. Leave to poach slightly for a couple of minutes.

Divide the spinach between two ovenproof dishes and spoon over the scallops and sauce.

Combine the remaining cheese with the breadcrumbs and sprinkle over the scallops.

Place on a baking tray and bake for 15 minutes – the sauce should be bubbling and the topping golden.

Serve with a green salad and warm crusty bread.

Caroline Ford
MATURE CHEDDAR & ENGLISH MUSTARD SCONES

///

These are delicious spread with plenty of butter while warm from the oven.

MAKES 6-8 SCONES

115g grated mature Cheddar cheese, plus extra for topping
1 tsp English mustard powder
225g self-raising flour
1 tsp baking powder
55g butter or margarine
1 egg and 5 tbsp whole milk, combined, plus extra milk for glazing
Pinch of cayenne pepper (or more if desired)
Good pinch of salt and black pepper

Caroline Ford, Swindon
"I entered this competition because I think it is a great idea. There are many people in the UK who enjoy cooking, who are not celebrities or professional cooks, so why not share some of their recipes? Some of my favourite recipes are ones that friends have shared with me. This scone recipe is one my mother used to make. What I love most about Lakeland is I know that I will get a quality product at a competitive price. I have never been disappointed with any of my Lakeland purchases."

METHOD

Preheat the oven to 220°C and line a baking tray with baking paper.

Sift together the flour, mustard powder, salt, cayenne and baking powder.

Use your fingers to rub together the butter or margarine and the flour mixture.

Use a fork to add the egg and milk mixture and the cheese, then get your hand in to bring the dough together.

Tip the dough onto a floured surface and bring together into a rough ball – do this quickly to avoid overworking the dough.

Roll out with a rolling pin dusted in flour until around 2cm thick, then use a 5cm/2-inch diameter cutter to cut out your individual scones.

Brush each scone with a little milk, then sprinkle with cheese and black pepper.

Transfer the scones to your baking tray and bake in your preheated oven for around 10 minutes, until lightly golden and risen to about double their original height.

When out of the oven, leave to cool slightly for five minutes, then break in half (you can usually pull the scones into two pieces with your hands, but if not use a serrated knife).

Cheryl Hockham
SMACKERS (HOMEMADE SMOKED MACKEREL PÂTÉ)

//

This is enough for six people. I made this as an experiment about 20 years ago as a first course before Christmas lunch. It is now a firm family favourite and our traditional starter.

SERVES 6

155g smoked mackerel (approx. 2 fillets)
70g sliced smoked salmon
150g cream cheese
200ml double cream
Squeeze of lemon juice

METHOD

Remove skin from mackerel.

Check carefully for any tiny bones and remove (I guarantee if I don't do this my husband gets a bone!).

Place in food processor and whizz until it becomes fine shreds (you can use a fork for this if you don't have a food processor).

Add the cream cheese and whizz again until combined.

Add the double cream and stir well, then squeeze in a little lemon juice and mix well.

Place in the fridge and allow to chill, usually overnight.

Slice the smoked salmon into pieces approximately 6cms square. Place approximately one teaspoonful of the mackerel mix onto the salmon and roll.

Alternatively, serve with thin slices of wholemeal bread and butter and a slice of lemon as pictured here.

Cheryl Hockham, Cannock
"I've been a Lakeland customer for at least 10 years now. I'm always impressed by the quality of their products, their customer service and their delivery service – if I order something after browsing online it's virtually always here the next day. And now my daughter is a fan of Lakeland too!"

David Aldred
ASPARAGUS WITH DIJON DRESSING & SESAME SEEDS

//

This is a vegan alternative to the usual starter of asparagus and parmesan shavings.

SERVES 3

15 stalks of asparagus
2 tsp Dijon mustard
2 tbsp tamari* or soy sauce
2 tsp white wine vinegar
2 tsp sesame oil
2 tbsp toasted sesame seeds (see note)

*Tamari is gluten-free

Note: Toast the sesame seeds in a wide frying pan on a medium heat for 3-5 minutes, shaking the pan occasionally. Remove the seeds when they darken and become fragrant. Allow to cool. Store them in a covered jar at room temperature

METHOD

To make the dressing, shake together the tamari or soy, mustard, sesame oil and vinegar in a clean jam jar.

Steam the stalks until they are just tender (5-6 minutes). Plate them up neatly, then drizzle the dressing over. Finally, sprinkle on the toasted sesame seeds.

David Aldred is a Lakeland customer from East Yorkshire.

The Hairy Bikers
SALMON, DILL & NEW POTATO TART

A celebration of everything summery, this tart is delicious served with a salad and a glass of home-made lemonade. It's a good way of making a small amount of salmon and smoked salmon go a long way too.

SERVES 6-8

For the filling:
2 x 150g fillets fresh salmon
200g new potatoes
200ml double cream
200ml crème fraîche
3 large eggs
100g smoked salmon, cut into strips
1.5cm wide
5 spring onions, sliced
1 small bunch of dill
Flaked sea salt
Freshly ground black pepper

For the shortcrust pastry:
250g plain flour, plus extra for rolling
150g cold butter, cut into cubes
1 large egg, beaten
You'll need a 25cm loose-based tart tin

With their irresistible enthusiasm, Si King and Dave Myers have become national treasures. Big hearted, down-to-earth cooks with a love of good food, they have been cooking together for more than 20 years. They have created haute cuisine dishes with Michelin-starred chefs and have travelled the world in the pursuit of great food.

METHOD

Preheat the oven to 200°C (fan 180°C). Wrap the salmon fillets in foil, put them on a baking tray and cook for 15 minutes. Leave to cool.

To make the pastry, put the flour and butter in a food processor and blitz on the pulse setting until the mixture resembles breadcrumbs. With the motor running, add the beaten egg and process until the mixture is just beginning to come together into a ball. Remove and shape the dough into a slightly flattened ball.

Roll out the pastry on a lightly floured surface to the thickness of a £1 coin and use it to line your tart tin. Trim the edges neatly.

Prick the base lightly with a fork and chill for 30 minutes. Bake the pastry case blind for 25 minutes. Carefully remove the paper and beans, then return the pastry to the oven for a further 5-10 minutes.

Meanwhile, cook the potatoes in salted, boiling water for 15-18 minutes, until tender but not too soft. Leave to cool slightly, then cut in half or into thick slices, depending on size.

Turn the oven down to 170°C (fan 150°C). Beat the cream, crème fraîche and eggs in a bowl and season. Flake the cooked salmon into chunks and arrange in the pastry case with the smoked salmon, potatoes and spring onions. Pour in most of the cream and egg mixture, then snip the dill over the top.

Put the tart on a baking tray and place in the oven, with the oven shelf pulled just a little, then pour in the rest of the filling and carefully push the oven shelf in. Bake for 35–40 minutes, until the filling is just set and the top is beginning to brown. Cool in the tin for 15 minutes before removing and serving.

Katy Goody
GIGI'S CHEESY NIBBLES

//

MAKES 25-30 NIBBLES

70g mature Cheddar cheese
1 tbsp Parmesan cheese
70g margarine
110g wholemeal flour
1 crumbled beef stock cube
Black pepper, to season

METHOD

Preheat the oven to 180°C.

Mix all the ingredients together in a mixer until they make a firm dough.

Form a roll.

Cut into thin discs, 10mm thick.

Place on a lightly oiled baking tray.

Bake for 15-20 minutes.

Cool on a wire rack.

Serve as party nibbles.

Katy Goody, Harpenden
"A few people had asked for this recipe after having the nibbles so I knew it wasn't just me that loves the biscuits. Unfortunately Gigi (my Gran) isn't with us any more so I just thought it would be nice to have her recipe included. She would have dined out on the story for a while and told everyone!"

Victoria Legge-Bourke, LVO
MAAAARVELLOUS MUSHROOMS

//

SERVES 6

*2-3 punnets of button or small
mushrooms – more than you think per
person as they shrink when cooked
250-300g butter
Generous tsp of mixed dried herbs
4-5 rashers of ready cooked crispy bacon –
roughly broken up
Small pot of single cream (approx.
150ml)
Splosh of brandy or sherry
2 large handfuls of grated strong Cheddar
or similar cheese
Salt and pepper, to season*

METHOD

Rush into the kitchen.

Grab the largest frying pan you have. Bung all the mushrooms in the pan – roughly slice any larger ones first. Put on a low heat with all the butter (cut into two large slices it will soon melt) and the mixed herbs. As the butter melts, the mushrooms will start to 'wilt' and give off liquid – turn from time to time until soft but not mushy. Crumble in the bacon bits and mix in. Throw in a big splosh of brandy or sherry. When it stops hissing, pour over most of the pot of cream. Season, but go easy on the salt as the bacon is quite salty.

Divide the mushrooms between six ramekin dishes, sitting in an oven tray (it's easier to handle when in a tin). Use the remaining liquid to cover the mushrooms – a few can still peep out at the top. Sprinkle the grated cheese over the top (enough to cover). At this stage you can leave out on the side and give yourself a glass of wine as a reward.

As the first guests arrive, stuff the tin containing the ramekins into a hot oven – about 200°C (I use the bottom shelf of the top right oven in my Aga) for about 20 minutes, until the cheese is bubbling and slightly browned. Give yourself another drink with your guests.

Serve ramekins piping hot on small plates with small brown bread rolls – homemade rolls are even better.

**Victoria Legge-Bourke
LVO, Gunthorpe, Norfolk**
"I've been a Lakeland customer for too long to remember. I get the catalogue and go online quite often. They offer very good value for money and their service turnaround is excellent. I entered the competition as a bit of fun – it appealed to me. I love cooking and do a lot of entertaining for friends."

Wendy-Ann Ensor

TOMATO & SHERRY SOUP

//

This soup was always a great favourite with my staff when I was teaching. They said that it gave them a warm glow during the afternoon so therefore I used to provide it two to three times a term!

SERVES 10

800g chopped firm plum tomatoes
4 tbsp olive oil
2 large red onions, peeled, quartered and finely chopped
4 large cloves garlic, peeled and finely sliced
1 tbsp tomato paste
Juice of 2 oranges plus zest of half
1 tbsp granulated sugar
2 tsp crushed coriander seeds
2 tsp chopped fresh basil
2 tsp Tabasco sauce
Splash of sherry
500ml vegetable stock
500ml milk
500ml single cream
Freshly ground black pepper, to season

For the garnish:
Double cream
Fresh basil leaves
Garlic croutons

METHOD

Heat the oil in a wok or deep pan and add the onions and garlic. Cook gently until soft and then add the tomatoes, tomato paste, grated rind and juice of the oranges, sugar, crushed coriander seeds and chopped basil. If you do not possess a mortar and pestle the coriander seeds may be crushed in a grinder. They will produce a sweet and spicy orange flavour to complement the oranges.

Simmer for approximately 25-30 minutes, stirring occasionally, until the tomatoes are soft. Add the Tabasco sauce to give a good piquant flavour and some black pepper, according to taste.

Gradually add the stock, milk, cream and sherry. The amount of liquid really depends on how thick you want your soup to be but I usually find that these quantities suit my guests. Strain through a fine sieve.

At this stage the soup may be frozen for up to six months.

Serve the soup hot, garnished with a swirl of cream, fresh basil leaves and garlic croutons.

Wendy-Ann Ensor, Chalfont St Giles, Buckinghamshire
"Over the past 20 years or so I have gradually been building up a collection of recipes in 'book form' for my own use. The 50th anniversary book sounded as if it deserved a contribution!"

MAIN COURSES

Ainsley Harriott
ITALIAN FUSILLI SAUSAGE 'RAGU'

//

This pasta dish is quick and easy to make and perfect for a cold winter's night. The 'ragu' or sauce seems to taste even better the next day, and makes a nice change from your average tomato-flavoured sauce.

SERVES 4

450g cocktail sausages
450g fusilli pasta (twists)
1 red pepper, halved, seeded and thinly sliced
1 yellow pepper, halved, seeded and thinly sliced
1 large red onion, thinly sliced
2 garlic cloves, crushed
1 tsp dried crushed chillies
120ml red wine
400g tin chopped tomatoes
1 tbsp sun-dried tomato pureé
2 tbsp olive oil
Salt and freshly ground black pepper

METHOD

Heat half the oil in a frying pan and sauté the sausages for about five minutes until lightly golden. Drain well on kitchen paper. Wipe out the pan and use to heat the remaining tablespoon of oil, then add the peppers and onion and sauté for five minutes until softened. Add the garlic and chillies and cook for another minute until well combined.

Meanwhile, plunge the fusilli into a large pan of boiling, salted water; stir once, then cook for 10-12 minutes until *al dente* or according to the packet instructions.

Return the sausages to the pan, pour in the wine and allow to bubble down. Add the tomatoes and tomato pureé, then season to taste. Cover with a lid and simmer for 8-10 minutes until slightly reduced and thickened, stirring occasionally. When the pasta is cooked, drain, rinse briefly if necessary, then fold the sausage mixture into the pasta. Season to taste and serve at once.

There are only a handful of personalities whose enduring popularity places them in that rare category where they are instantly recognised simply by their first name. 'Ainsley' can only mean Ainsley Harriott. He's the master of fresh, fun, accessible cuisine. Alongside his TV career, Ainsley is also a No.1 bestselling author.

Angela Heather
RICH VENISON CASSEROLE WITH MUSTARD MASH

///

SERVES 6

1kg venison, diced
2-3 tbsp seasoned flour
75-100g streaky bacon, cut into small pieces
250-375ml red wine
150g chestnut mushrooms, sliced or quartered
2-3 carrots, chopped
2 sticks celery, chopped
2 onions, finely chopped
1-2 cloves garlic, crushed
50g dried cranberries
Rind of 1 orange
10-15 juniper berries
2 tbsp redcurrant jelly
Small glass of port
Few drops Worcestershire sauce
2 bay leaves
2 sprigs thyme
Oil, for cooking
Salt and pepper, to season

For the mustard mash:

600g potatoes, peeled and cut into chunks
75ml double cream
75g butter
1½ tbsp wholegrain mustard

METHOD

Heat the oven to 130°C.

Put the seasoned flour in a food bag, then add the diced venison and shake until it's fully coated.

Heat up some oil in an ovenproof cooking pot, brown the venison in batches, and then set aside.

Add some more oil to the pot, and sauté the bacon.

After a couple of minutes, add the celery, onion and carrot, fry until softened, then add the garlic and fry a little more.

Return the venison to the pot and add all the other ingredients including the liquids. The less liquid you use the richer the sauce will be, but make sure you cover the meat.

Put a lid on the pot and stick it in the oven for a couple of hours, checking occasionally to give it a stir and add a little water if it starts to dry out.

Put potatoes in a pan and cover with water. Add one teaspoon of salt. Simmer for about 20 minutes until cooked. Drain and mash, adding a knob of butter and some cream. Beat well, add the mustard and adjust seasoning.

★ This tastes particularly good the next day when reheated. It also freezes well.

Angela Heather, Hungerford
"I have been a Lakeland customer for probably 40 years; Lakeland has the answers to all my cooking projects – it is the sort of shop that I never come out of empty-handed."

Angela Wiggins
CARIBBEAN SALTFISH CURRY

SERVES 4

300g salted cod or white fish
2 tbsp sunflower or other oil (not olive oil)
1 onion, sliced
1 Scotch Bonnet chilli, finely chopped and deseeded
¼ each green, red and yellow peppers, sliced
2 fresh tomatoes, diced
4 tbsp mild curry powder
4 garlic cloves, crushed
1 tsp ginger (grated if fresh)
1 chicken stock cube
1 tbsp paprika
Pinch all purpose seasoning
¼ cup hot water
Dash soy sauce

METHOD

If using salted cod, soak overnight then drain.

Place the drained fish into a pan of boiling water (no salt). Bring to the boil, simmer for 20 minutes then drain.

Prepare all the other ingredients. Fry the onions in oil until soft, add the garlic, ginger and chilli and fry for one minute, stirring. Add the curry powder and paprika and fry for a further minute, stirring. Add the drained fish and stir gently to cover with spices. Add the peppers and cook for two minutes, stirring gently. Add the tomatoes and stir in gently. Sprinkle in the stock cube and all purpose seasoning and stir gently. Add the water and stir gently.

Cover and cook on a low heat for 20 minutes.

Add a dash of soy sauce, taste and add more if needed.

Cook through for one minute.

Serve with rice and peas, or boiled dumplings Caribbean style.

Angela Wiggins, Banbridge
"I feel Caribbean food should be prized for its flavour and simplicity. This recipe reminds me of my late mother and my childhood – she would cook it on a Saturday or Sunday on special request, served with dumplings or savoury rice and plaintain. It is fairly healthy and low in fat with a good use of vegetables, great flavour and not too expensive to make."

Lakeland customer, Oxfordshire
MOTHER'S PHEASANT WITH PORT, CELERY & CREAM DEDICATED TO MARY PICKERSGILL

//

SERVES 4

1 pheasant
175ml port
1 head celery, chopped
175ml cream
110g butter
2 rashers streaky bacon, chopped
275ml chicken stock
1 egg yolk
Salt and pepper, to season
1 tbsp parsley, chopped (optional)

METHOD

Heat the butter in a casserole pan and brown the pheasant, turning for approximately 10 minutes.

Add the port, bacon, salt and pepper and stock and simmer for 30 minutes with the lid on.

Add the celery and simmer for another 40 minutes, or until the pheasant is cooked.

Take the pheasant, celery and bacon out of the pan and keep warm.

Reduce the stock by boiling for 15 minutes. Remove from the heat.

Add the egg yolk and cream (stirred together).

Return the stock to the heat and stir gently without boiling.

Serve decorated with the parsley (optional).

"I decided to enter the competition in recognition of my mother's superb cooking and baking skills. She was a farmers' wife from Yorkshire and loved sharing her food with family and friends. I know she would have been pleased to share and give pleasure to other like-minded cooks. My mother took me to the flagship Lakeland store when it was first opened in Ambleside and I have subsequently introduced her granddaughter to Lakeland."

Name not revealed by request

Barry Shandley
SMOKED FISH PIE

//

MAKES 4 INDIVIDUAL PIES

750g smoked haddock or cod
750g potatoes, peeled
300ml milk to poach the fish in, plus a
little extra for later cooking
1 large onion, finely chopped
100g mushrooms, sliced
25g flour
25g Cheddar cheese, grated
15g butter
2 hardboiled eggs, chopped
Juice and grated rind of 1 lemon
1 bay leaf
1 tbsp chopped parsley
1 tbsp chopped chives
¼ tsp cayenne pepper
Salt and freshly ground black pepper, to
season

METHOD

Poach the fish in the 300ml of milk, seasoned with black pepper and bay leaf, for 10-15 minutes. Drain, retaining the cooking liquid.

Boil the potatoes, mash and add a little of the butter, milk and seasoning. Allow to cool. Lightly fry the chopped onion and sliced mushroom until just softened.

Make a white sauce by melting the remaining butter, add the flour and cook for about a minute. Allow to cool slightly before gradually adding the retained cooking liquid (made up to 300ml with extra milk if necessary). Bring slowly to the boil, stirring constantly, and season well. Flake the fish, taking care to remove all bones, and add to the sauce with the mushroom, onion, parsley, chopped egg, lemon juice and rind, cayenne pepper and chives.

Season well, spoon into a 900ml pie dish. Sprinkle the grated cheese over the top. Pipe mashed potato over the fish mixture, using a 1cm star vegetable nozzle. Bake in a moderately hot oven for 20-30 minutes. Serve with peas and baked tomatoes.

For a luxury touch, add prawns, chopped smoked salmon pieces and scallops to the fish mixture!

Barry Shandley, Clacton-on-Sea
"I decided to enter the competition as a tribute to my late wife, Pamela, who introduced our family to this dish. It was always very well received and I have been making it regularly since her death in 1993. I have been a Lakeland customer for very many years. What I love most about Lakeland is the huge range of innovative products available uniquely from them."

Brian Turner

ROAST SPICED FILLET OF BEEF
WITH ROAST PICKLED ONION YORKSHIRE PUDDING, BRAISED SWEDE & ENGLISH MUSTARD & HORSERADISH CREAM SAUCE

SERVES 4

700g piece centre cut fillet
of beef (21 days hung)
50g dripping
1 tsp chilli flakes
1 tsp garlic salt
1 tbsp chopped and dried
parsley
¼ tsp curry powder
12 pickled onions, medium
sized
1 tsp vegetable oil
25g butter
50g dripping (reserved from
earlier)
450g swede
75g butter
1.2 litres chicken stock
Salt and pepper

For the Yorkshire puddings:
110g flour
110g eggs
110g milk/water
1 pinch salt
1 tbsp malt vinegar

For the sauce:
25g butter
1 shallot, chopped
140ml white wine
70ml Madeira
150ml meat stock
150ml double cream
¼ tsp English mustard
1 tbsp horseradish cream
sauce
1 tbsp chopped parsley

Brian Turner is one of
Britain's best-known chefs.
He has become a successful
television personality, after
appearing regularly on
'Ready Steady Cook'. Brian
was the Chairman of the
Academy of Culinary Arts for
11 years and since 2004
President. In 2002 he was
awarded a CBE for his
services to tourism and
training in the catering
industry.

METHOD

Tie the fillet with string to keep
its shape. Heat the dripping and seal the outside. Take off the heat and allow to cool – do not throw away the dripping.

Put the chilli into a coffee grinder, then add the other spices and parsley and grind to a fine powder. Roll the beef in the spices to cover all sides, season with salt then roll in clingfilm and leave for three hours.

Put into the oven in the tray used to seal the meat at 180°C for 10 minutes. Turn the oven down to 160°C, turn the meat over and cook to your required temperature/liking. Take out and keep warm.

Meanwhile, for the Yorkshire puddings, make the batter by mixing together the flour, eggs, milk/water, pinch of salt and malt vinegar, then pour into very hot small muffin trays with the dripping preheated and bake in the oven at 210°C for approximately 25 minutes. At the same time, colour the onions in the oil, add the butter, season and cook in the oven at 210°C for 10 minutes. When cooked take both out and keep warm.

Shape the swede into one large piece per person. Colour one side in 50g melted butter. Turn over, season, add the chicken stock and bake in the oven at 180°C, brush with more melted butter during cooking. Take out and keep warm.

Make the sauce by melting 25g butter, add the shallots, sweat but do not colour. Add the wine and reduce by two-thirds, add the Madeira and reduce by one-third. Add the meat stock and reduce by half. Add the cream and boil till starting to thicken. Take off the heat, add the mustard and horseradish and strain into a clean pan. Check the seasoning, then add the parsley.

Carve the beef into four steaks and put in the middle of the plates.

Put the onions into the Yorkshire puddings and place round the beef.

Put the swede on the plates and swirl sauce around the plate, serve some separately.

Celia Davidson
BAVARIAN BEEF ROLLS

//

SERVES 4

8 thin slices lean beef eg. sirloin
2 medium onions, chopped
4 rashers unsmoked bacon, chopped
1 large pickled gherkin, chopped
1 tbsp olive oil
1 tbsp tomato pureé
1 cup beef stock
1 tbsp flour
1 tsp caraway seeds
½ bottle dry red wine
German mustard
Salt and freshly ground black pepper, to season

METHOD

Spread each beef slice with a generous amount of mustard and season with the salt and pepper.

Top with a mixture of the chopped onion, bacon and gherkin and roll up firmly in the beef before securing the rolls by either tying with string or by using cocktail sticks to skewer them together.

Heat the oil in a medium pan and sauté the rolls until browned all over.

Add the other ingredients to the pan, cover and simmer gently until tender (approximately one hour).

Taste and add further seasoning if required.

Serve two rolls per portion with rice or creamed potato for a hearty main course.

Celia Davidson, Ayrshire
"I enjoy cooking and I have lots of recipe books. I like to bring back recipes from places I've been and do my own interpretations of them – this recipe is an example of that. I've been a Lakeland customer for over 10 years, since it was called Lakeland Plastics. They have got lots of innovative ideas and good quality products, both kitchen and household."

Hazel Milcoy
GIOUVETSKI (A GREEK LAMB DISH)

//

This is a perfect dish for entertaining as it is all cooked in one pot and can be prepared well in advance. I first discovered it on the island of Samos and as I could find no recipe I played around until I got it right. You can use chicken or beef, which they do on Corfu, but lamb just melts in the mouth. I used to have to bring orzo pasta back from Greece with me but now you can get it in any big supermarket – it works much better than any other type.

SERVES 4

Lamb, cubed – leg, fillet or even shanks
2 onions, chopped
2 cloves garlic, finely chopped
2 red peppers, chopped
Olive oil, for frying, or whichever oil you prefer to fry in
200g Halloumi cheese, cubed
350g Orzo pasta
2 tsp ground cinnamon, or to taste
2 tsp ground cumin, or to taste
2 tsp oregano, or to taste
Small pinch of ground cloves – optional, but it is traditional
680g passata
750ml stock – I usually use lamb stock made with two cubes, or homemade chicken stock if I have it.
Red wine or brandy, to taste – optional but nice!
Salt and pepper, to season

Hazel Milcoy, Surrey
"I just had to enter this competition because Lakeland has been a part of my life for so long – right back to the days when it was Lakeland Plastics. In fact, my husband sometimes calls me Mrs Lakeland! It is wonderful to pass on my love of baking."

METHOD

Brown the meat in a pan with oil – I use a large casserole pot that will go on the hob and into the oven. If using shanks, I cook the dish and then strip the meat off the bone before serving.

Leave the meat aside and fry onions and peppers in the oil until softening. Add the garlic and spices.

Return the lamb to the pot and add the passata and stock.

Cook in the oven on a low heat (170°C or lower) until the meat is fully cooked – about 2-3 hours.

Add the orzo to the pot – you may need a little more stock as the pasta will absorb the liquid. I add wine and/or brandy at this stage.

Return the casserole to the oven until the pasta is cooked. You can thicken the sauce with extra passata if needed but usually the pasta absorbs enough to thicken it.

10 minutes before serving, stir the Halloumi cheese through the dish. Don't be tempted to leave this out – it really makes the dish!

It only needs a green salad to serve with it.

Jane Langton
CHICKEN STUFFED WITH GOATS' CHEESE, SERRANO HAM & TOMATO

Chicken breasts can be much more interesting if stuffed and rolled, especially as the cooking method I use helps them to stay moist and succulent. There are various options for the stuffing, but my favourite is goats' cheese with Serrano ham and a few basil leaves.

SERVES 4

4 chicken breasts, skinless
4 slices Serrano ham
1 packet of soft goats' cheese
1 small jar of tomato pesto
12 fresh basil leaves
1 tbsp olive oil
1 tbsp butter
Salt and pepper, to season

Jane Langton, La Bruguiere, France

"In 2010 I retired and with my husband we renovated an old stone house in the Languedoc and now run a B&B (*Chambre d'Hotes*). So now I finally have time to focus on my cooking! I have been using Lakeland products for over 20 years and am delighted that I can continue to be a customer whilst living in France. With Lakeland I can always find what I need, so I love the innovation, consistent quality and great service."

METHOD

First beat out each chicken breast until it is about 1.5cm thick. To do this place the chicken breast on a board, season, cover with a piece of clingfilm and beat gently with a rolling pin, making sure you don't make any holes in the meat.

Spread each chicken breast with one teaspoon of tomato pesto and then place a piece of Serrano ham on top. Place three basil leaves in a line at one end and spread four tablespoons of soft goats' cheese on top. Starting at the top by the goats' cheese, roll the chicken into a cylindrical shape.

Wrap the chicken breasts in clingfilm so they are tightly sealed and tie securely at each end. Place them in a large saucepan of simmering water, completely covered, and simmer for 10 minutes.

In a sauté pan, add the olive oil and butter. Remove the chicken from the clingfilm wrapping and sauté for five minutes until a nice golden brown, basting regularly with butter and oil.

To serve:
Slice the chicken breasts diagonally into thick slices and serve with dauphinoise potatoes, a chicken and masala jus, haricot beans and a few roasted cherry tomatoes.

Jemma Fielding
KING PRAWN LINGUINE WITH CHILLI, GARLIC & ASPARAGUS

SERVES 4

1 packet of large king prawns (200g)
1 bundle of asparagus (300g)
3 large cloves of garlic
2 green bird's eye chillies
2 dried red chillies
250g dried linguine
5 tbsp olive oil
Salt and black pepper, to season
Parmesan cheese, to serve

METHOD

A couple of hours before you want to serve, chop half the garlic into thin slices and crush the other half.

Chop the bird's eye chillies, leaving in the seeds if you want the dish to be very hot.

Gently fry the garlic, chilli and dried chillies in the olive oil for around two minutes, taking care not to burn the garlic, then take off the heat and leave for a couple of hours to infuse.

When you are ready to eat, prepare a bowl of cold water and ice. Prepare the tips of the asparagus by snapping in half to get rid of the woody ends. Place the asparagus tips in a pan of salted boiling water and cook for two minutes. After two minutes, remove from the boiling water using a slotted spoon and place immediately into the iced water. This will stop the cooking process and ensure that the asparagus stays bright green and crisp.

Place the asparagus on a paper towel to remove all excess water.

Season the prawns with salt and pepper.

Add more water to your pan, bring to the boil and add salt. Add the dried linguine and a drop of oil to prevent sticking. Boil the pasta without a lid for around 10 minutes until the pasta is *al dente* (not too hard but not too soft).

When the pasta is almost done, warm your oil and gently fry your king prawns and asparagus for a few minutes in the garlic and chilli oil until the prawns are warmed through. If using raw prawns add before the asparagus and cook until pink. Remove your dried chillies.

Take your pasta from the pan, drain well then add to the frying pan with your prawns and asparagus. Toss until the pasta is coated thoroughly in the oil and the prawns are distributed evenly.

Salt to taste.

Serve in a large bowl with freshly ground black pepper and a touch of Parmesan cheese.

Jemma Fielding, Ashton-under-Lyne
"I have been receiving the Lakeland catalogue for about six years now. I love the kitchen gadgets that make life easier! I had just tried this recipe and thought it was really nice, so it seemed appropriate to share!"

Heston Blumenthal
TRIPLE-COOKED CHIPS

///

I became obsessed with chips around 1992, before I had even opened the Fat Duck, and this was probably the first recipe that I could call my own. It has since cropped up in restaurants and pubs all over the place. Achieving the crisp, glass-like exterior depends on getting rid of moisture from the potato and creating little cracks in the surface where the oil will collect and harden, making it crunchy.

SERVES 6

1kg Maris Piper potatoes, peeled and cut into chips (approx. 2 x 2 x 6cm)
Groundnut or grapeseed oil
Sea salt

METHOD

Place the cut chips into a bowl under running water for five minutes to wash the starch off.

Place two litres of cold tap water in a large saucepan and add the potatoes. Place the pan over a medium heat and simmer until the chips are almost falling apart (approximately 20-30 minutes, depending on the potato).

Carefully remove the cooked chips and place them on a cooling rack to dry out. Then place in the freezer for at least one hour to remove more moisture.

Heat a deep-fat fryer or a deep pan no more than half filled with oil (to a depth of around 10cm) to 130°C. Fry the chips in small batches until a light crust forms (approximately five minutes), remove from the oil and drain on kitchen paper.

Put the potatoes on a cooling rack and place in the freezer for at least one hour. (At this stage, if you don't want to cook and serve immediately, the chips can be kept in the fridge for three days.)

Heat the oil in the deep-fat fryer or deep pan to 180°C and fry the chips until golden (approximately seven minutes). Drain and sprinkle with sea salt.

Entirely self-taught, Heston Blumenthal is the most progressive chef of his generation. In 2004 he won the coveted three Michelin stars in near-record time for his restaurant The Fat Duck, which has twice been voted the Best Restaurant in the World by an international panel of 500 experts.

Michel Roux Jr
FAISAN ARCHIDUC
(PHEASANT STUFFED WITH TRUFFLE & FOIE GRAS)

This is real cuisine bourgeoise – rich, opulent and satisfying. The cooking method ensures a moist and flavoursome bird and this recipe also works well with guinea fowl.

SERVES 2

1 hen pheasant
Thin slices of pork back fat
½ onion, peeled and chopped
40g long-grain rice
80ml chicken stock
100g cooked foie gras, diced (optional)
60g shelled pistachios
2 tbsp game jus
60g cooked truffles, diced
4 tbsp Malmsey Madeira wine
200ml double cream
1 tbsp vegetable oil
1½ tbsp unsalted butter
Salt and black pepper

Michel Roux Jr is one of London's most respected chefs. Le Gavroche, which he has run since 1991, continues to receive recommendations for excellence in every food guide. Michel's early training in France instilled in him a belief in simplicity and quality of raw ingredients which has he put to use in developing the recipes he uses both at Le Gavroche and in his books.

METHOD

First prepare a rice pilaf for the stuffing. Preheat the oven to 200°C (fan 180°C) Place an ovenproof pan on the hob, melt half a tablespoon of the butter and sweat the onion until softened. Add the rice and stir to coat all the grains in butter, then pour in the chicken stock. Bring to the boil, then transfer the pan to the oven and bake for 20 minutes. Remove and set aside for 20 minutes.

When the rice is cool, gently mix in the foie gras, then add the pistachios, game jus and diced truffles. Season well.

Remove the wishbone from the pheasant and stuff the bird with the rice mixture, which should fill the cavity. Truss the bird to seal the neck and rear. Cover the bird with the slices of back fat and tie them securely in place.

Preheat the oven to 200°C (fan 180°C). Heat the oil and remaining butter in a casserole dish and, when hot and foaming, add the bird and colour it on all sides. Place the dish in the oven with the bird breast-side up. After 10 minutes, add a spoonful of Madeira and put the lid on the casserole. Repeat this until the bird has been cooking for 40 minutes, then take the dish out of the oven, remove the fat and set the bird aside to rest.

Add the cream to the casserole dish and any juices that have run from the bird, then season. Put the dish on the hob, bring the liquid to the boil and reduce to a sauce consistency, then pass through a fine sieve. Spoon out the stuffing and carve the bird. Serve with the sauce, stuffing and some seasonal vegetables, such as braised cabbage.

Michelle Cain
SHELL'S ONE POT GARLIC CHICKEN

//

SERVES 4

1.8kg chicken
8-10 merguez (spicy lamb) sausages
450g new potatoes
3 peppers – a mixture of red and yellow
2 courgettes
8-10 shallots
1 bulb garlic, split into cloves and peeled
(optional)

For the marinade:
6 cloves garlic, crushed
Large pinch saffron
1 tbsp ground coriander
Zest of 1 lemon
A few sprigs thyme leaves, shredded
1 tbsp honey
2 tbsp olive or rapeseed oil
1 small glass white wine
Black pepper, to season

METHOD

Mix all marinade ingredients and baste all over the chicken – leave for at least four hours.

Wash and halve the new potatoes.

Chop the pepper and courgettes into large chunks.

Peel the shallots but leave whole.

Line a baking tray with the veggies. Place the chicken on top.

Arrange the sausages around the chicken.

Pour over white wine.

Cover with foil.

Bake in the oven at 170°C for 2½ hours.

Uncover for the last 30 minutes to brown the chicken and vegetables.

Serve with steamed green veg and warm crusty bread to mop up the juices.

Michelle Cain, Tollesbury
"Even when my husband's coffee machine broke down after 18 months, Lakeland's 'no quibble' guarantee replaced it. I entered the competition because I love to cook and create – it is my relaxation along with gardening. My husband never knows what my next creation will be!"

Paul Hollywood
SAUSAGE PLAIT

// ////

SERVES 6

Shop-bought puff pastry (enough to make a rectangle about 26 x 30cm)
300g chestnut mushrooms, trimmed
2 tbsp thyme leaves
1 tbsp sunflower oil
25g unsalted butter
2 red onions, thinly sliced
2 tsp soft brown sugar
1 tbsp sherry vinegar
300g good-quality sausagemeat (or skinned butcher's sausages)
100g black pudding, cut into 1-2cm pieces
1 tbsp sesame seeds
Salt and pepper

METHOD

Wrap the puff pastry in clingfilm and chill in the fridge while you prepare the filling.

Put the mushrooms in a food processor, season with salt and pepper and pulse until reduced to a rough paste. Add the thyme and give the mix a final pulse. Transfer to a dry frying pan and cook over a medium-high heat, stirring often, until all the liquid has evaporated from the mushrooms. Remove from the pan and set aside to cool.

Heat the oil and butter in a wide frying pan on a medium-low heat. Add the onions with the sugar and cook slowly until soft and lightly caramelised. This will take at least 20 minutes. Stir in the sherry vinegar and set aside to cool.

Heat your oven to 200°C. Line a large lipped baking sheet with baking parchment (some butter may leak out of the pastry).

Roll out the pastry to a rectangle, about 26 x 30cm. Spread the mushroom paste down the middle third of the pastry, leaving a 5cm gap at the top and bottom.

Mix the sausagemeat with the black pudding, mould into a long sausage shape that will fit on top of the mushroom paste and place it on the paste. Spread the caramelised onions on top of it.

Cut slits on the diagonal all the way down the pastry on each side of the filling at 2cm intervals. Brush lightly with egg. Take one strip over the filling from one side, then one from the other and so on, crossing the strips over to form a plaited effect. Tuck the ends of the pastry under the plait, trimming off excess if necessary. Using a large palette knife, carefully lift onto the prepared baking sheet.

Brush the plait with beaten egg and sprinkle with sesame seeds. Bake for 30 minutes or until the pastry is golden brown. Leave to settle for 10 minutes or so, then serve hot or cold. This is delicious with a dollop of apple sauce on the side.

The son of a baker, Paul has been a judge on The Great British Bake Off (for three series) and Junior Bake Off, all alongside Mary Berry.

//// //

Pip Vickery
STEAK LAREDO

//

SERVES 4

900g braising steak, sliced
250ml beef stock
2 tbsp cooking oil
1 medium onion, finely sliced
6 tbsp water
6 tbsp tomato ketchup
1½ tbsp Worcester sauce
½ tsp Tabasco sauce
½ level tsp salt

METHOD

Heat the oil in a saucepan, add the steak and onion and lightly fry for a few minutes.

Stir in the beef stock, water, tomato ketchup, Worcester sauce, Tabasco sauce and salt.

Cover tightly and simmer very gently for about an hour or until the meat is tender, stirring occasionally.

Pip Vickery is a Lakeland customer from Kent.

Rick Stein
MADRAS FISH CURRY OF SNAPPER, TOMATO & TAMARIND

///

I have nominated this as my favourite curry. I've used the same fish it was cooked with on that day in Mamallapuram – snapper – but in the UK I recommend using any of the following: monkfish fillet, because you get firm slices of white, meaty fish; filleted bass, preferably a large fish, because although you'll get softer flesh it has plenty of flavour; or gurnard. I think more than anything else that this dish typifies what I was saying about really fresh fish not being ruined by a spicy curry. I can still remember the slightly oily flavour of the exquisite snapper in that dish because fish oil, when it's perfectly fresh, is very nice to eat. I always think oily fish goes well with curry anyway, particularly with the flavours of tomatoes, tamarind and curry leaves.

SERVES 4-6

700g snapper fillets, cut into 5cm chunks
1 tbsp yellow mustard seeds
1 large onion, finely chopped
3 cloves garlic, finely crushed
30 fresh curry leaves
2 tsp Kashmiri chilli powder
2 tsp ground coriander
2 tsp turmeric
400g tin chopped tomatoes
100ml Tamarind liquid
2 green chillies, each sliced lengthways
into six pieces, with seeds
60ml vegetable oil
1 tsp salt

METHOD

Heat the oil in a heavy-based saucepan or karahi over a medium heat. When hot, add the mustard seeds and fry for 30 seconds, then stir in the onion and garlic and fry gently for about 10 minutes until softened and lightly golden.

Add the curry leaves, chilli powder, coriander and turmeric and fry for two minutes, then stir in the tomatoes, tamarind liquid, green chillies and salt and simmer for about 10 minutes until rich and reduced.

Add the fish, cook for a further five minutes or until just cooked through.

Serve with boiled basmati rice.

Rick Stein is a well-loved and respected chef, TV presenter and author who has produced an array of award-winning books and television series. He divides his time between Padstow and Australia, which he regards as his second home.

Rosemary Shrager
CHICKEN & POTATO PIE

// ////

This is my famous chicken and potato pie, which I've made countless times. It's my family's favourite dish and if I had to choose a last meal this would probably be it. The trick is to make sure the potato is very well-seasoned, otherwise it can be bland. It's a rustic dish, to be placed in the centre of the table so that everyone can help themselves. I once cooked 36 of these pies for a friend's wedding, one on each table.

SERVES 4

4 large skinless, boneless chicken breasts, cut into thin strips
750g potatoes, thinly sliced
800g puff pastry
130g unsalted butter, plus extra for greasing
3 shallots, finely chopped
2 tbsp tarragon leaves
2 tbsp chopped chives
Flour for dusting
2 egg yolks, lightly beaten, for glazing
240ml double cream
Sea salt and black pepper

METHOD

Put the potatoes and half the butter into a pan and heat gently, turning from time to time, until they are just tender but not brown. Transfer them to a large bowl and set aside to cool.

Meanwhile, soften the shallots in the remaining butter. Add the herbs and chicken, turning the mixture over a steady heat for a few minutes until the meat is partially cooked. Add to the bowl of potatoes, mix carefully and season well with salt and pepper. Set aside to cool.

Place half the pastry on a lightly floured work surface and roll it into a circle about 30cm wide. Transfer it to a lightly buttered baking sheet. Brush the perimeter of the pastry with beaten egg yolk, then pile the chicken mixture in the middle.

Roll the remaining pastry into a circle about 36cm wide and place it over the filling, sealing and crimping the edges. Cut a circle about 10cm wide in the top, but leave it in place; this will act as a lid. Brush the whole surface with the remaining egg yolk.

Bake in an oven preheated to 180°C for about 50 minutes, checking that it's not browning too much, in which case lower the heat slightly.

When the pie is ready, heat the cream until boiling, then season with salt and pepper. Carefully remove the small pastry lid from the pie and pour in the cream, lifting the mixture gently to allow it to circulate. Put the lid back on and return the pie to the oven for 10 minutes.

Rosemary is a talented and versatile chef and cookery teacher, who loves talking about food as much as she loves cooking. Her professional career includes a period working for Pierre Koffmann.

Sue Thersby

REMOSKA BAKED SQUASH & STILTON RISOTTO

//

SERVES 2

½ butternut squash, peeled and cubed
1 tbsp olive oil
1 onion, chopped
25g butter
150g risotto rice
400ml vegetable stock
115g Stilton
Parmesan cheese, to garnish

METHOD

Bake the squash in a Remoska cooker for 25-30 minutes in a little olive oil, then remove.

Cook the onion in butter in the Remoska for 10-15 minutes.

Add the rice and stir round until it is coated.

Add the vegetable stock and cook for about 25 minutes or until the rice is cooked.

Add the Stilton and squash.

Serve with grated Parmesan cheese.

Sue Thersby, Cheadle Hulme, Cheshire
"Happy birthday Lakeland! We go back a long way together – I reckon it must be 35 of those 50 years. I love Lakeland because of the range of goods it offers and the advice and helpfulness of the staff at our local branch in Handforth. I decided to enter the competition, as I love cooking with my Remoska both at home and in France in our caravan, as it is so easy."

Tom Kitchin
ROASTED RACK OF VENISON WITH SPICED RED CABBAGE

SERVES 4

1kg rack of roe deer venison on the bone
Vegetable oil for cooking
Sea salt and freshly ground black pepper
50g butter
1 thyme sprig

For the spiced red cabbage:
½ medium-large red cabbage
Olive oil for cooking
½ onion, peeled and sliced
2 star anise
1 cinnamon stick
Pared zest and juice of 1 orange
50g soft light brown sugar
50ml white wine vinegar
400ml red wine
100ml port
50g sultanas
1 dessert apple

To serve:
Redcurrant or rowanberry jelly

METHOD

First, prepare the cabbage. Cut out the core and finely shred the cabbage. Heat a heavy-based saucepan over a medium heat and add a generous drizzle of olive oil. Add the onion and sweat for 2-3 minutes, then add the cabbage and cook for 1-2 minutes. Add the star anise, cinnamon and some salt and pepper and cook for another 1-2 minutes to release the flavours.

Now add the orange zest and sprinkle in the sugar. Add the orange juice and wine vinegar and let it bubble to reduce down. Pour in the red wine and port. Add the sultanas and leave to cook gently for 40 minutes. Peel, core and dice the apple. Add to the cabbage, toss to mix and set aside.

Meanwhile, for the venison, heat the oven to 200°C. Heat a large non-stick ovenproof frying pan over a medium heat and add a drizzle of oil. Season the venison joint on both sides with salt and pepper and place in the hot pan. Colour the meat well on all sides for about three minutes. Add the butter to the pan and let it melt and foam, then add the thyme and baste the joint with the foaming butter.

Transfer the pan to the oven. Roast the venison for 15 minutes, then check; the meat should still be pink inside. Transfer to a warm platter and leave to rest in a warm place for 10 minutes. Save any juices in the pan.

Slice the venison and arrange on warm plates with the braised cabbage. Reheat any pan juices and drizzle over the meat. Add a spoonful of redcurrant jelly and a sprinkling of pepper to serve.

Tom Kitchin demonstrates a culinary CV that extends from early training at the Gleneagles Hotel to experience garnered from some of the world's most renowned chefs and restaurants. Tom is Scotland's youngest Michelin-starred chef proprietor, having achieved a star aged only 29, and has become a well-known face on television.

Wendy McConville
CELEBRATION QUICHE

//

SERVES 8-10

For the pastry case:
225g plain flour
55g butter
55g lard

For the filling:
1 tbsp oil
1 medium-sized cooking onion
4 rashers bacon
1 tbsp Dijon mustard
110g strong Cheddar cheese, grated
1 tomato
285ml double cream
5 eggs
Salt, to season

Note: Use more tomato and bacon according to preference.

METHOD

For the pastry case:
First weigh out the flour and cut the butter and lard into small pieces. Rub the butter and lard into the flour, and when it resembles fine crumbs add cold water a drop at a time, bringing the breadcrumbs to a soft dough. Refrigerate for an hour wrapped in clingfilm.

Line a 25cm/10-inch fluted flan case with the dough and refrigerate again for another hour. Cut a 35cm circle of greaseproof paper or baking parchment to line the pastry case and fill with baking beans.

Bake in the oven at 180°C for 15 minutes then remove the paper and beans, prick the base all over with a fork and put back into the oven for a further 10 minutes.

For the quiche filling:
While the pastry case has been chilling, make the filling. In a large non-stick frying pan heat the oil, finely slice the onion and fry until soft and golden. Add the bacon and fry on a medium heat until cooked through. Turn off the heat and add the Dijon mustard. Leave the mixture to cool.

When the pastry case is cool, which will only take 15 minutes, sprinkle the cheese over the base then sprinkle the bacon, onion and mustard mixture over the top of the cheese.

Beat the five eggs and mix into the double cream. Season with a pinch of salt (not too much because the bacon can tend to be salty). Pour over the cheese, onion and bacon. Slice the tomato and lay the slices on top of the cream mix, then put into a preheated oven at 160°C for approximately 45 minutes. You will know when it is ready because it will rise and turn a golden colour.

This can be enjoyed hot or cold.

Wendy McConville is a Lakeland customer from Coventry.

////

PUDS

Cathie Wells
WHITE CHOCOLATE & TANGERINE MOUSSE

///

I made this up about five years ago and everyone who tries it asks for the recipe!

MAKES 8

300g white chocolate
200ml double cream
200ml Greek yoghurt
1 tangerine jelly (23g pack)
298g tin mandarins
Milk chocolate, to melt over the top
(optional)

METHOD

Melt the white chocolate in the microwave, stirring every 30 seconds then leave to cool slightly.

Whip the double cream and yoghurt until stiff.

Melt the jelly with one tablespoon of water in a microwave. Add the juice from the tin of mandarins and any extra water needed to make the juice up to 400ml.

Stir the jelly and white chocolate into the cream and yoghurt.

Mix well to ensure an even colour and texture is obtained.

Pour into serving bowls and refrigerate for at least four hours.

If required, some tangerines can be added to the mousse as it sets. Otherwise use the mandarin pieces to decorate on top of the mousse once set.

If required, drizzle melted milk chocolate over the top for a professional finish.

Cathie Wells is a Lakeland customer from Buckinghamshire.

Eric Lanlard
PEAR TARTE TATIN

SERVES 6

225g puff pastry or 375g pack ready-rolled puff pastry, chilled
Plain flour, for dusting
50g unsalted butter, softened
100g golden caster sugar
2 tbsp Poire William liqueur or lemon juice
4-6 ripe pears
1 tsp juniper berries

To serve:
Crème fraîche or fromage frais

Tip: Lift the fruit using a knife to check that it is caramelised right through before adding the pastry. It should take on a dark caramel colour within 10-15 minutes and feel bouncy when pressed.

Eric is an award-winning master patissier and international baking star. He is the author of five books – his latest 'Chocolat' is an exquisite collection of his stunning recipes, celebrating his favourite ingredient.

METHOD

Preheat the oven to 220°C (fan 200°C). Have ready a 24cm (9½-inch) tarte tatin dish, or ovenproof omelette pan.

Roll out the pastry on a lightly floured surface. Then, using a plate that is slightly larger than your pan, cut out a circle of pastry. Lightly prick with a fork and chill while you prepare the remaining ingredients.

Using your fingers, press the butter onto the base of your pan until it coats it evenly. Sprinkle the sugar over the butter and set aside.

Place the liqueur in a large bowl. If you don't want to use alcohol, add lemon juice instead, which will help prevent the fruit discolouring.

Prepare the pears one at a time. Peel, cut into quarters and cut out the cores. Toss in the liqueur or lemon juice.

Place the tarte tatin pan on a medium-high heat. Watch the pan carefully at this stage, moving it around if one area is browning faster than another. As soon as the sugar has caramelised, remove from the heat. Scatter the juniper berries into the caramel.

Take the pears from their juice and tightly pack in a circle in the pan, ensuring that their more attractive rounded sides are pressed lightly into the caramelised sugar. Place on a medium-high heat. The pears will shrink slightly as they cook, so do not be afraid to add another pear half or two. Keep cooking for 10-15 minutes until the pears are a nice dark caramel colour.

Take the pan off the heat and quickly press the pastry circle on to the top of the pears, tucking the edges down the side of the pan, then place in the centre of the preheated oven. Bake for 25 minutes or until the pastry is a beautiful golden colour and well risen. Do not worry if some of the caramelised juices bubble out.

Remove from the oven and leave to sit for five minutes. Then take a warm serving plate, press against the pastry and invert the pan, giving a good shake. The tart should slip out, juices and all. Serve with lots of crème fraîche or fromage frais.

Gail Ford
CHOCOLATE VELVET PUDDINGS

//

Suitable for a romantic meal for two. I made this for my husband on our first wedding anniversary and it was an instant hit. It is now a firm favourite.

SERVES 2

30g caster sugar
60ml cold water
90g plain chocolate (70% cocoa solids)
1 egg
1 tbsp brandy (alternatively use dark rum or Grand Marnier depending on your own taste)
60ml double cream

Gail Ford, Chesterfield
"I entered the competition on impulse as soon as I read about the 50th anniversary recipe book that Lakeland were planning. I have been a regular customer since being a teenager when I first became interested in cooking. The first time I made this recipe was for my husband on our first wedding anniversary so it's a favourite of ours. We've been married for 22 years this year so maybe it's the recipe to success."

METHOD

Place the caster sugar and water into a small pan over a gentle heat until the sugar is all dissolved.

Break the dark chocolate into pieces.

Bring the syrup to the boil, remove it from the heat and add the chocolate pieces, stirring until melted.

Break the egg into a bowl and pour over the chocolate mixture. Whisk with a handheld electric mixer or a balloon whisk for one minute. The heat from the chocolate will be sufficient to cook the egg.

Add the brandy (or alcohol of your choice).

Lightly whip the cream and fold this into the chocolate mixture.

Transfer the mixture to two ramekins or glass dishes of your choice and chill for at least two hours but if time allows, overnight. Decorate with chocolate shavings, a sliced strawberry, crunchy amaretti biscuit or biscotti. The choice is yours.

Sit back and enjoy!

Gregg Wallace
CHERRY & CHOCOLATE CAKE

Do you make cakes? Are you scared of them?
You shouldn't be. Follow these instructions
and, I promise you, you will become a top cook overnight.

SERVES 8

55g blanched almonds, toasted
55g plain flour
125g Divine 70% dark chocolate
3 tbsp water
3 medium eggs, separated
125g butter, softened
125g caster sugar

For the topping:
400g cherries, stoned
4 tbsp rum or brandy
Divine 70% dark chocolate shavings

For the ganache:
225g Divine 70% dark chocolate, broken
into pieces
450ml double cream

Gregg is a writer, media personality and former greengrocer. He is probably best known for co-presenting MasterChef, Celebrity MasterChef and MasterChef: The Professionals.

METHOD

For the topping: Place the stoned cherries in a small bowl with three tablespoons of the rum or brandy. Leave to soak overnight.

Preheat the oven to 180°C. Grease a 23cm/9-inch springform tin and line with baking parchment. Whizz the almonds and flour together in a food processor until the nuts are finely ground.

Melt the 125g chocolate with the water in a bowl over simmering water. Take off the heat and beat in the egg yolks with the remaining tablespoon of rum or brandy. Set aside.

Beat the butter and sugar together until light and fluffy. Stir in the chocolate mix, and then gently fold in the flour/almond mix. Whisk the egg whites until soft peaks from. Gently fold this into the cake mix.

Pour into the prepared tin and bake for 30–35 minutes, until cooked through. Remove from the oven and leave in the tin for 10 minutes. Turn out of the tin on to a wire rack and leave to cool completely.

For the ganache: Put the chocolate pieces in a large bowl. Bring the cream to the boil and pour over the chocolate. Leave for about five minutes, by which time the chocolate should have melted. Mix together and leave to cool.

With an electric mixer, beat the ganache until lighter in colour and very thick. Put the cold cake back in the clean springform tin. Pour over the cherries and alcohol. Spoon over the ganache, and smooth the surface. Cover with clingfilm and chill for at least two hours before serving. Remove the outside of the tin before doing so.

Decorate with chocolate shavings. Simply use a potato peeler along the side of a bar of chocolate to make these.

Helen Hutton
LEMON MERINGUE ROULADE

//

SERVES 8

For the meringue:
5 egg whites
140g caster sugar
1 level tsp cornflour

For the filling:
300ml double cream
2 tbsp lemon curd
1-2 tbsp lemon juice

Icing sugar for dusting

METHOD

In a large bowl whisk the egg whites until stiff. Add three quarters of the caster sugar one tablespoon at a time, whisking well after each addition. Whisk in the remaining sugar and cornflour. Turn into a lined Swiss roll tin, levelling the meringue.

Bake for 45 minutes at 130°C (fan oven).

Remove from the oven and leave to cool in the tin.

For the filling, whip the cream until soft peaks form, then fold in the lemon curd and lemon juice to taste.

Turn the meringue out onto parchment paper liberally dusted with icing sugar, peel off paper and spread the filling over the meringue.

With one short edge facing, gently roll into a log, then, using the paper to help lift the roulade, transfer to a serving dish.

Helen Hutton, Edinburgh
"I have been a customer of Lakeland since I got married 29 years ago when the company was known as Lakeland Plastics. At the time I was living in the countryside and loved browsing through the mail order catalogue. Baking tins purchased then were used for our children's christening cakes and more recently two daughters' wedding cakes. Now living in Edinburgh I take great pleasure in shopping in the Lakeland stores where there are so many innovative, interesting and unusual kitchen and home products."

Jacqueline Lundy
DOUBLE CHOCOLATE NUTTY ROULADE

//

SERVES 4-6

For the meringue:
5 egg whites
170g caster sugar
1 tbsp cornflour

For the filling:
250ml double cream
3-4 tbsp Nutella spread
85g chopped hazelnuts
15 marshmallows, chopped
15 Maltesers

Alternative filling:
250ml double cream
4-5 tbsp Baileys
Mint Matchmakers, chopped

METHOD

Whisk the egg whites, and whisk in the sugar and cornflour until stiff. Pour into a Swiss roll tin.

Cook at 100°C for one hour.

Whip the cream and add the Nutella, nuts, marshmallows and Maltesers.

Spread onto the meringue and roll. Decorate with dusted cocoa.

Jacqueline Lundy, Co. Derry, Northern Ireland
"Lakeland is one of my favourite shops that I'm always recommending to friends. The products are of excellent quality and value. I always look forward to the catalogue, as there are always new products to choose from. I decided to enter the competition because I love sharing recipes. This dessert is always a winner, especially with all those who love chocolate!"

James Martin
ICE BOX CAKE

// ////

This is my favourite pudding in my book. I first tried it at the Magnolia Bakery in New York City (made famous by Sex and the City), and loved it so much I now make it at home. I hide the biscuit packet, though! The show's not really my thing (no cars or guns), but the cakes are great. The idea is that New York ladies are short on time, so they make this with a few ingredients, then put it in the ice box (in other words, the fridge) for a while to soften the biscuits into a cake texture – hence the name. I sometimes like to use soft fruit in the cream, but a coffee cream also works well with ginger biscuits.

SERVES 10-14

400g raspberries (optional)
2 litres double cream
70 chocolate biscuits

METHOD

Crush the raspberries, if using, through a sieve to make a smooth purée.

Whip the cream to loose, soft peaks and fold through the raspberry purée to create a marbled effect.

Place seven biscuits in a circle formation on a cake stand, cover in a layer of the raspberry cream, making sure the biscuits are still visible at the sides. Top with another layer of biscuits.

Repeat the process until you have used up all the biscuits, and finish with a layer of cream. Serve immediately, or chill in the fridge for a few hours and serve very cold.

Presenter of the BBC's Saturday Kitchen, James Martin is one of the UK's most popular TV chefs, and his enthusiasm and passion for food have won him countless fans. His accessible approach to cooking has been showcased in his numerous books including Desserts (2007) and Slow Cooking (2012).

//// //

Jenny Welch
BANOFFEE ICE CREAM

SERVES 4-6

4 large eggs, separated
110g caster sugar
285ml double cream
1 soft banana, mashed
8 fudge or toffee sweets
A little milk

METHOD

Whisk the egg whites until stiff, gradually adding the sugar and whisking all the time.

Add the egg yolks and mix and then fold in the lightly whipped cream.

Add the mashed banana.

Soften the fudge or toffee sweets over heat with a little milk. Cool and add to the ice cream mixture.

Freeze for at least 12 hours in a large container. This ice cream does not need to be beaten during freezing time and makes a soft creamy ice cream.

Serve with chocolate sauce.

**Jenny Welch,
Hemel Hempstead**
"I discovered Lakeland about 15 years ago, originally using the catalogue for postal orders, but now the Watford store has become my local kitchen and cooking emporium. I entered the competition as I am a keen cook and like to share my recipes."

Jo Wheatley
GIANT MALTESER CUPCAKE

//

SERVES 4

300g self-raising flour
200g caster sugar
100g soft light brown sugar
300g Stork or unsalted butter, softened
6 medium eggs, beaten
60g cocoa powder
100g Greek yoghurt
1 regular packet of Maltesers, roughly crushed

For the buttercream:
300g unsalted butter, softened
600g icing sugar
2 tbsp Horlicks
2 tbsp Ovaltine

To decorate:
Family-size packet of Maltesers (crush 16 with a rolling pin)
2 packets of Cadbury White Chocolate Fingers

You will also need a giant cupcake tin, greased with cake-release spray or a flavourless cooking oil such as sunflower or rapeseed, a piping bag fitted with a plain nozzle, and raffia or a ribbon to decorate. I use the Nordic Ware tin, which has a 'cake base' and 'frosting lid'

METHOD

Preheat the oven to 170°C.

Add the flour, sugars, butter and beaten eggs to the bowl of a free-standing mixer and beat until combined. Add the cocoa powder and beat until combined. Fold in the yoghurt and crushed Maltesers using a large metal spoon.

Pour the batter into the prepared tin halves and bake on the middle shelf of the preheated oven for one hour to one hour 20 minutes or until a skewer inserted into the middle of the cakes comes out clean. Leave to cool in the tin for 10 minutes, then turn out onto a wire rack and cool completely.

To make the buttercream, beat the butter, icing sugar, Horlicks and Ovaltine in a freestanding mixer until light and fluffy.

Sandwich the two cake halves together with a third of the buttercream and the crushed Maltesers. Spread a thin layer around the sides of the base of the cake and stick the chocolate fingers to this to create the cupcake case. Spoon the remaining buttercream into the piping bag, then form a swirl on the top half of the cupcake and decorate with the remaining Maltesers. Tie a little raffia around the base to secure the chocolate fingers.

Since winning The Great British Bake Off, Jo has set up a small cookery school from her home in Essex. She has also published two books, A Passion For Baking and Home Baking.

John Whaite
CHOCOLATE BERRY FRAISIER CAKE

//

SERVES 4-6

For the genoise sponge:
4 eggs
130g golden caster sugar
110g plain flour
20g cocoa powder
50g unsalted butter, melted and cooled slightly

METHOD

Preheat the oven to 200°C (fan 180°C) and place a 20cm cake ring, that is 6cm deep, onto a baking sheet lined with baking paper.

For the genoise sponge: The cake is best done in a freestanding electric mixer with whisk attachment, but if you don't have one then use a clean metal bowl and a handheld electric whisk. Place the eggs and sugar in the bowl and whisk until they triple in volume and reach the ribbon stage – when you lift the whisk out of the bowl and draw a figure eight, the ribbon should sit proud on the surface for a few seconds.

Sift together the flour and cocoa powder into a bowl, then gently sprinkle over the surface of the whisked eggs and sugar. With a flat spatula or large metal spoon, gently fold the flour into the eggs, ensuring that you scrape right to the bottom of the bowl too, but try not to deflate the mixture.

When the flour is just about incorporated, pour the melted cooled butter down the side of the bowl and fold that in too. Gently pour this mixture into the ungreased cake ring, and bake for about 25 minutes, or until a skewer inserted into the centre comes out clean. Remove from the oven, turn the cake ring upside down on a cooling rack, and allow to cool.

John Whaite is a British baker, cook and TV personality. He studied Patisserie at Le Cordon Bleu in London, and has published his first book, John Whaite Bakes: Recipes for Every Day and Every Mood. Gaining a first class degree in Law from the University of Manchester after declining a place to study at Oxford University, John decided to hang up the gown and don the apron, a decision spurred on after he won the third series of the BBC's The Great British Bake Off.

Continued on next page...

For the crème patissiere:
4 egg yolks
125g golden caster sugar
40g cornflour, plus extra for dusting
500ml milk
1 vanilla pod, halved lengthways or 1 tsp
vanilla paste or extract
40g unsalted butter

For the blackcurrant crème mousseline:
2 tbsp crème de cassis
175g unsalted butter, cubed and chilled
slightly
75g white chocolate, melted and cooled

For the soaking syrup:
50g golden caster sugar
2 tbsp kirsch
½ tsp lemon juice

METHOD (CONTINUED)

For the crème patissiere: Place the egg yolks and caster sugar in a mixing bowl and whisk until the sugar is dissolved and the mixture is slightly paler in colour.

Add the cornflour and whisk well so there are no lumps of flour left. Place the bowl on a folded, dampened tea towel in readiness for the next stage.

Put the milk in a medium saucepan along with the vanilla and place over a medium to high heat until just before the milk boils. Pour half the milk into the bowl with the eggs, whisking continuously as you do so. The dampened tea towel helps stop the bowl sliding around.

When the milk is well incorporated into the eggs, pour it all back into the remaining milk in the saucepan and return to a medium high heat, whisking constantly until the mixture is bubbling gently and is thick enough to coat the back of the spoon, barely dripping off. This will take 3-4 minutes.

Remove from the heat, continue to whisk for a minute more, then add the butter, stirring until it is melted into the crème patissiere. Remove the vanilla pod, if you used one. Pour the crème patissiere into a bowl, allow to cool briefly, then cover the surface with clingfilm, to prevent a skin forming, and refrigerate until cold.

For the blackcurrant crème mousseline: Put the crème patissiere into a mixing bowl and beat it to slacken it. Do this in the freestanding electric mixer with the whisk attachment or in a mixing bowl with a handheld electric whisk. Once the crème patissiere is loosened beat in the crème de cassis liqueur, then slowly add the butter, then the white chocolate. Scrape into a bowl, cover with clingfilm and refrigerate.

For the soaking syrup: Heat together the sugar and 50ml water. Bring to the boil and allow to boil for a minute or two. Remove from the heat and stir in the kirsch and lemon juice.

Free the cake by scraping a knife around inside the cake ring and lifting it off. Slice the cake horizontally into two even slices, and set aside. Clean the cake ring and place it on top of a 20cm cake stand or serving plate. Take the slice of cake that was the top and place this top side down into the cake ring. Soak it well with about half of the syrup, using a pastry brush to avoid completely drowning the cake.

For the berry filling:
400g strawberries (try to get smaller, even-sized ones)
150g blackberries (get the biggest ones you can)

For the topping:
2 tbsp blackcurrant jam
50g marzipan

For the mirror glaze:
1 leaf of gelatine
120g golden caster sugar
1 tbsp golden syrup
75g cocoa powder
60ml single cream
Gold leaf, to decorate

For the berry filling: Take the most perfect strawberry and set it aside, then chop off the leafy ends of the rest, to create a flat bottom. Slice each strawberry in half down the length so that you can see the inside. Cut each blackberry in half this way too. Align the fruit against the sides of the tin: take a strawberry half and place it flat-bottom on to the layer of cake, cut middle pressed against the side. Place a blackberry half in the same way next to it, then alternate the fruits all the way around the circumference, gently squeezing them together so they stay in place.

Chop the remaining fruit roughly, and place it in a bowl. Put the crème mousseline into the piping bag and pipe a spiral from the centre outwards onto the cake, ensuring you pipe in and amongst the berries at the edge – you won't need all of the mousseline at this point.

Pile the remaining chopped fruits into the centre of the mousseline spiral, then pipe the remaining mousseline over the top. Smooth off with the back of a spoon. Take the second layer of cake, and place this cut-side down on to the mousseline, so that the original flat bottom of the cake is now the top. Press down ever so gently, then soak that in the remaining syrup.

For the topping: Paint the blackcurrant jam onto the surface of the cake, then roll out the marzipan to a circle the size of the cake – use a little dusting of cornflour to prevent the marzipan sticking. Place this gently on top of the jam, so that it sticks to the cake. Place into the fridge while you make the mirror glaze finish.

For the mirror glaze: Soak the gelatine leaf in a bowl of cold water for five minutes.

Heat the sugar, 60ml water and golden syrup in a small saucepan. Allow to boil for a minute or two, then remove from the heat and whisk in the cocoa powder. Whisk in the cream, then return to a medium heat for a minute, stirring constantly. Remove from the heat.

Take the gelatine leaf from the bowl, squeeze to remove excess water, add to the chocolate glaze and stir until dissolved. Pass the glaze through a sieve into a bowl.

Allow the glaze to cool for just a minute so that it is still pourable. Pour enough glaze over the cake to cover the surface of the marzipan, but don't let it drip down the sides. Return the cake to the fridge and allow to cool for at least two hours.

When ready to serve, gently warm the cake ring by rubbing your hands around it then delicately lift up off the cake. Press gold leaf on to the perfect strawberry you reserved earlier, place on top, and serve. To retain the neat edges, cut with a sharp knife dipped in hot water.

Laura English
SALTED CARAMEL & BANANA CHEESECAKE

//

SERVES 4

For the base:
90g butter
250g crushed chocolate digestive biscuits

For the filling:
400g cream cheese at room temperature
120g caster sugar
400ml whipping cream (chilled)
1 tin caramel (Carnation is good)
15g rock salt
1 banana
1 tsp granulated sugar

Note: to make neat portions when slicing, use a hot sharp knife, dipped in hot water and cleaned after every slice.

Laura English, Blaydon on Tyne
"I have my grandmother to thank for introducing me to Lakeland. She shopped here and inspired me to bake. I love the excellent, fresh ideas that I wouldn't have thought about myself. It makes life much easier! I decided to enter the competition because I love baking and I wanted to share and hopefully encourage others to bake too!"

METHOD

Melt the butter in a saucepan over a low heat and leave to cool.

Crush the biscuits and mix together with the melted butter.

Press the crumbs evenly and firmly into the base of a spring form/loose based 23cm/9-inch tin.

Beat the cream cheese with an electric whisk for a few minutes until smooth.

Slowly add the caster sugar and whisk on a low speed.

Once the sugar is dissolved, add the cream slowly, pouring down the bowl. Mix on a low setting.

Once it is all combined turn the mixer on high. The mix should hold its shape and start to look slightly grainy.

Add half of the tin of caramel to a saucepan and simmer. Once bubbles form, remove from the heat, stir in the rock salt until dissolved and allow to cool.

Mix the caramel with the cream cheese. Don't combine – just mix it slightly to make a marbled effect.

Spoon the mixture onto the base and smooth out.

Stand in the fridge to set.

Pour the rest of the caramel in a frying pan and simmer. Chop the banana into slices and add to the pan.

Brown the bananas off. Take the pan off the heat and allow them to soak in the caramel.

Take the bananas out of the pan and place on top of the cheesecake. Pour the caramel out of the pan and drizzle over the cake. Sprinkle the bananas with the granulated sugar.

Chill for at least four hours or overnight.

Lindsey Winterton
NANCY'S ALMOND DELIGHTS

This was one of my late mum's favourite recipes; it is a real family favourite. I have never found a similar recipe anywhere. These little tarts with a macaroon type topping really melt in the mouth. It is a delightful confection for a celebratory afternoon tea. A lovely variation to this recipe can be made at Christmas by substituting mincemeat for the jam.

MAKES 18-20 DELIGHTS

For the pastry:
255g self-raising flour
140g margarine
3 egg yolks
A little water

For the filling:
Raspberry jam – homemade is best!
110g ground almonds
280g icing sugar
3 egg whites
½ tsp almond essence

METHOD

Make the pastry by combining all the ingredients and cut out rounds to line bun tins.

Put a small teaspoon of jam in each pastry case.

Mix together the icing sugar and ground almonds.

Whip the egg whites and fold them into the mixed icing sugar and ground almonds. Add in the essence.

Cover the jam with a good spoonful of this mix.

Bake at 180°C (fan 155°C) for 20-25 minutes.

Enjoy!

★ *Be mindful of them sticking to the sides. Perhaps line your bun tins with silicone paper or use cake liners.*

Lindsey Winterton
"Sadly Nancy, my mother, died in 2012, aged 98, and I went through all her recipe cards and notebooks and made a recipe book for the family. Of all the recipes, I think this was her favourite, and she would have been absolutely thrilled that it was included."

Lorraine Pascale
WHITE CHOCOLATE & PISTACHIO SPONGE BLONDIES

MAKES 16 BITE-SIZED SQUARES OR 8 RECTANGULAR BARS

75g unsalted butter
150g white chocolate, roughly chopped
3 eggs
Seeds of ½ a vanilla pod or ½ tsp vanilla extract
75g caster sugar
3 tbsp plain flour
1 tsp baking powder
Pinch of salt
100g strawberries, hulled and chopped into 1cm cubes
50g green pistachio nuts, roughly chopped
Spray oil

Tired of prancing around in front of the camera, former model Lorraine realised a dream with her first television cookery series 'Baking Made Easy' being launched as a prime time TV show on BBC2. She enrolled at the world-famous Leith's School of Food and Wine then worked in a string of top restaurants, culminating in a spell in the US with Peggy Porscher, cake decorator to the stars.

METHOD

Preheat the oven to 170°C (fan 150°C). Grease a 20cm square cake tin with a little spray of oil and then line it with baking parchment. I just cut a long strip of paper to cover the bottom and come up on opposite sides of the tin with the excess hanging over a little. This makes it easier to lift the baked cake out of the tin.

To prepare the blondies, melt the butter in a small pan over a low heat. Then remove from the heat, add the white chocolate and set aside to allow it to melt.

Put the eggs and vanilla seeds or extract in a large bowl and, using a hand whisk or a mixer fitted with a whisk attachment, give them a good whisk up. They will become really light, fluffy and mousse-like. Add the sugar and keep whisking. The sugar will make the eggs increase in bulk even more. To test if the eggs are whisked up enough, use a spoon to pick up some of the egg mixture and then drop it back down. If they are whisked up enough, the spoonful will sit on the surface for about five seconds (if it sits for longer, that's brilliant too!) before disappearing back into the mixture. Once the egg mixture reaches this stage, it is ready.

Give the now-melted chocolate a little stir into the butter to blend and pour it around the edges of the egg mixture. Do this from a low height so you don't knock out all of that wonderful air which you have just beaten in. Then, using a spatula, fold them together, scooping right down to the bottom of the bowl, as the chocolate tends to sink down there. Sprinkle the flour, baking powder and salt over and fold the mixture in using as few 'folds' as possible so you keep all that air in, but enough folds to make sure there are no lumps of flour in there. Finally, gently fold in the strawberries and pistachios.

Gently pour the mixture into the prepared tin from a low height and level it out with the back of a spoon. Bake for 30-35 minutes until a knife inserted into the centre comes out clean. Once cooked, remove from the oven and leave to cool in the tin. It will collapse in the centre a little, but don't worry – it will taste great. Once cooled, carefully remove from the tin, peel off the paper and cut into eight rectangular bars or 16 bite-sized squares and serve. The pistachios will sink to the bottom along with the strawberries – all meant to happen and all very tasty.

Mary Berry
ALL-IN-ONE VICTORIA SANDWICH

This must be the best-known and loved of all family cakes. The all-in-one method takes away the hassle of creaming, and ensures success every time. Baking spreads give an excellent result, but the cake won't keep as long.

SERVES 8

For an 18cm/7-inch Victoria Sandwich, use:
3 large eggs
175g softened butter
175g caster sugar
175g self-raising flour
1½ tsp baking powder

For a 15cm/6-inch Victoria Sandwich, use:
2 large eggs
100g softened butter
100g caster sugar
100g self-raising flour
1 tsp baking powder

For the filling and topping:
4 tbsp strawberry or raspberry jam
A little caster sugar, for sprinkling

Great British Bake Off judge Mary Berry trained at The Cordon Bleu in Paris and Bath School of Home Economics. In the swinging sixties she became the cookery editor of Housewife magazine, followed by Ideal Home magazine. In 2012 she had the honour of receiving a CBE.

METHOD

Pre-heat the oven to 180°C (fan 160°C). Grease your sandwich tins then line the base of each tin with baking parchment.

Measure the butter, sugar, eggs, flour and baking powder into a large bowl and beat until thoroughly blended. Divide the mixture evenly between the tins and level out.

Bake in the pre-heated oven for about 25 minutes or until well risen and the tops of the cakes spring back when lightly pressed with a finger. Leave to cool in the tins for a few minutes then turn out, peel off the parchment and finish cooling on a wire rack.

When completely cold, sandwich the cakes together with the jam. Sprinkle with caster sugar to serve.

★ *For 15cm/6-inch cakes, bake for 20 minutes.*

Raymond Blanc
APPLE TART 'MAMAN BLANC'

In my book, Maman Blanc makes the best apple tart. It takes its roots from simplicity. The secret lies in choosing the right apple, with a great flavour and the right balance of acidity and sweetness. The varieties I have suggested to use here will fluff up and caramelise beautifully, filling your kitchen with an enticing apple aroma. I sometimes pour a light custard into the tart towards the end of cooking – it is simply divine, so do try it. I also make this tart using other fruits, notably plums, apricots and cherries.

SERVES 6

For the shortcrust pastry:
200g plain flour
100g unsalted butter, diced, at room temperature
1pinch of sea salt
1 organic/free-range medium egg
1 tbsp cold water

For the apple filling and glaze:
3 dessert apples, such as Cox's Orange Pippin, Worcester, Egremont Russet, Braeburn
15g unsalted butter
15g caster sugar
1½ tsp lemon juice
7g Calvados (optional)
Icing sugar, for dusting

METHOD

To make the shortcrust pastry:

Put the flour, butter and salt into a large bowl and rub together delicately using your fingertips until the mixture reaches a sandy texture[1].

Create a well in the centre and add the egg and water. With your fingertips, in little concentric circles, work the liquid ingredients[2] into the flour and butter mixture; then at the last moment when the eggs have been absorbed, bring the dough together and press to form a ball[3].

Turn onto a lightly floured surface and knead gently with the palms of your hands for 10 seconds until you have a homogeneous dough; do not overwork it.

Break off 20-30g dough, wrap separately and chill. Wrap the remaining dough in clingfilm and flatten it to about a 2cm thickness. Leave to rest in the fridge for 20-30 minutes[4].

Place the rested dough in the middle of a large sheet of clingfilm, about 40cm square, and cover with another sheet of clingfilm, of similar dimensions. Roll out the dough to a circle, 2-3mm thick[5].

Continued on next page…

Totally self-taught, Raymond Blanc is one of the world's most respected chefs. His hotel Le Manoir aux Quat'Saisons in Oxford has been awarded two Michelin stars for the past 26 years.

[1] *For a successful pastry you need to have even distribution of butter within the flour, to give it flakiness. This is difficult to achieve if the butter is cold, so make sure it is at room temperature. Rub in delicately with your fingertips; do not try to knead at this stage.*

[2] *At this point it is for you to judge the consistency of the dough. If it is too wet add a little flour; if too dry add a little water. Flours differ in their absorbency.*

[3] *Alternatively, you could make the pastry in a food processor, using the pulse button to bring the dough together.*

[4] *Because you have worked the gluten in the flour, the dough is elastic at this stage. Resting it in the fridge makes the dough more pliable and easier to roll. This will minimise shrinkage in the oven.*

[5] *Rolling the dough between clingfilm enables you to roll it very thin without using flour. You then discard the top layer, using the bottom clingfilm to pick up the pastry. As you place the pastry in the tart ring ensure the clingfilm is uppermost.*

[6] *Pricking the base will help the distribution of heat and thorough cooking.*

[7] *A common problem is an undercooked, soggy base – the result of insufficient bottom heat. Using a bottomless tart ring and a baking stone overcomes this, as there is an instant transfer of heat from the hot baking stone to the pastry base.*

METHOD (CONTINUED)

To line the tart ring:
Place the tart ring on a wooden peel or flat tray lined with greaseproof paper. Lift off the top layer of clingfilm from the pastry and discard, then lift the dough by the lower clingfilm and invert it into the tart ring, removing the clingfilm. Press the dough onto the base and inside of the ring with the little ball of dough, ensuring that the pastry is neatly moulded into the shape of the ring.

Trim the edge of the pastry by rolling a rolling pin over the top of the ring.

Now, push the pastry gently up by pressing between your index finger and thumb all around the edge of the tart ring, to raise the edge 2mm above the ring.

With a fork, prick the bottom of the pastry case[6]. Place in the fridge for about 20 minutes to relax the pastry.

To prepare for baking:
Preheat the oven to 220°C. Place a baking stone[7] or baking tray on the middle shelf of the oven.

Peel and core the apples and cut each one into 10 segments. Lay the apple segments closely together and overlapping in a circle in the base of the tart case. In a small pan, melt the butter and sugar, then remove from the heat and mix in the lemon juice and Calvados, if using. Brush this mixture over the apple slices and dust liberally with icing sugar.

To bake the tart:
Using the peel or board, slide the tart directly onto the preheated baking stone or tray in the oven and cook for 10 minutes. Turn the oven down to 200°C and bake for a further 20 minutes until the pastry is light golden in colour and the apples are beautifully caramelised. Leave the tart to stand for about 30 minutes before serving, until barely warm. To de-mould, remove the ring and slide the tart onto a large, flat plate.

Dust with icing sugar to serve.

Variation:
For a creamy filling, whisk one medium egg with 50g caster sugar and 100ml whipping cream to make a light custard and pour into the tart 10 minutes before the end of cooking.

SEASONAL

Alison Motley
RASPBERRY, HAZELNUT & FRAMBOISE CHOCOLATE BROWNIES

//

These are a 'grown up' version of chocolate brownies, very rich and decadent and converted me to becoming a dark chocolate lover! They are great as an after dinner dessert with cream or as an adult party treat.

MAKES 16

185g good quality dark chocolate (I use Green and Blacks 70% cocoa)
185g unsalted butter, diced
3 large free range eggs
275g golden caster sugar
85g plain flour
40g cocoa powder (I use Green and Blacks Organic)
75g fresh raspberries
75g roughly chopped toasted hazelnuts
1 tbsp framboise liqueur

METHOD

Preheat the oven to 180°C (fan 160°C.

Grease and base line a 20cm square cake tin (or use a silicone cake pan).

Melt the chocolate with the butter over a gentle heat in a large saucepan.

Whisk the eggs and sugar together until thick and creamy and double their volume.

Add the cooled chocolate mix and fold in gently.

Sift in the flour and cocoa and fold in gently.

Finally gently stir in the hazelnuts and framboise.

Pour half the mixture into the tin, sprinkle over half the raspberries, pour over the remaining mixture and gently push the remaining raspberries into the top of the mixture.

Bake for 25-30 minutes until the top is papery. Leave to cool in the tin.

Remove when cold and cut into square – this makes 16, or 32 smaller triangles!

Alison Motley, Chelmsford
"I have shopped at Lakeland, both mail order and in store, for as long as I can remember. I have always loved cooking and enjoy inventing and adapting recipes. Whenever I make these brownies I get requests for the recipe so I thought it would be fun to share it and see what others think of it."

Angela Jones
PEPPER & LIME GINGER CAKES

//

MAKES 12 CAKES

For the ginger cakes:
90g butter
150g light muscovado sugar
2 large eggs
175g self-raising flour
1 tsp baking powder
6 pieces stem ginger chopped
175ml hot water

For the icing:
200g butter
200g soft cheese
450g icing sugar
Grated rind of 2 limes
1 tbsp black pepper, milled
Couple of drops fern green food colouring
12 chocolate cigarillo twirls, for decoration
(optional)

Angela Jones, Liverpool
"I love Lakeland because it is a place I can go and lose myself deciding which baking essential to buy next. They always come up with new stuff to keep us interested. I entered this competition as I enjoy experimenting with my baking and this particular recipe was a bit different and delicious. I tried it out on my friends and it was a big hit!"

METHOD

For the ginger cakes:
Preheat the oven to 180°C.

Cream the butter and sugar together in a bowl.

Add the eggs.

Add the flour and baking powder.

Beat until smooth.

Add the ginger.

Add the water.

Mix well.

Pour the mix into 12 cupcake cases.

Put in the oven for 20 minutes until cooked.

For the icing:
Mix the butter, soft cheese and icing sugar together until soft and fluffy.

Add the grated lime rind to the buttercream.

Add the tablespoon of black pepper (or more if you're brave enough) and green food colouring.

Mix well with a hand mixer.

Once the cakes are fully cooked, pipe the cream onto the cakes with your favourite piping nozzle.

Add a chocolate cigarillo twirl into each cake for effect (optional).

//

Ann Jakubowiak
RICH POLISH CHOCOLATE GATEAU

//

SERVES 4

For the cake:
4 eggs
110g caster sugar
110g ground almonds
110g plain chocolate
110g whole blanched almonds (optional)

For the topping:
285ml double cream
1 tbsp rum or brandy
Cake crumbs (see points 3 and 5 of method)

For the icing:
110g plain chocolate
1 tbsp black coffee
10g butter

METHOD

Put the eggs and sugar into a large bowl and whisk until thick – the mark of the whisk should show in the mixture.

Melt the chocolate in a bowl over hot water. Fold the ground almonds into the eggs and sugar mix, followed by the melted chocolate.

Put three-quarters of the mixture into a greased sandwich tin. Put the rest into a small greased tin to use for crumbs.

Bake the small cake in the top of the oven at 180°C for approximately 25 minutes. Cook the large cake for 45 minutes – watch carefully that it does not scorch.

The next day, make crumbs from the small cake.

Whisk the cream until just stiff then fold in the rum or brandy and cake crumbs.

Spread smoothly over the top of the large cake.

Melt the chocolate for the icing with the coffee and butter in a bowl over hot water.

Allow the icing to cool but remain soft, then spoon over the whole cake, spreading this to show little patches of cream.

Decorate with almonds (optional).

Ann Jakubowiak is a Lakeland customer from Stockton-on-Tees.

Anne Jones
ROSE & PISTACHIO CAKE WITH WHITE CHOCOLATE GANACHE

SERVES 8

170g caster sugar
170g butter
170g self-raising flour
3 eggs
300ml double cream
200g good quality white chocolate
3-4 tbsp raspberry jam
50g pistachios, chopped
Few drops of rose essence
Few drops of pink food colouring
3 whole fresh strawberries, for decoration

Anne Jones, Bromsgrove
"I work as a Teaching Assistant in a primary school and I love sharing ideas and recipes with my colleagues, and even making simple delightful bakes with the children. Cakes and pastries aside, my biggest passion is baking and decorating biscuits. I have been a passionate Lakeland customer ever since I moved to the Midlands in 1986 when I visited the store at Stratford-upon-Avon for the first time. I even remember my very first purchase which was a set of three coloured bottles and 2 x 8-inch cake pans which I still use to this day!"

METHOD

Cream the butter and sugar until pale and fluffy. Beat in the eggs one at a time until they are all incorporated. With the third egg, add a spoonful of sifted flour also. Fold in the remaining flour, add a few drops of the rose essence and pink food colouring and mix until completely incorporated. Divide the mixture into two prepared 20cm/8-inch cake pans and bake at 200°C for 20-25 minutes. The cake should be well risen and an even colour all round. Remove from the oven and turn out onto a cooling wire. Allow the sponges to cool completely, for at least an hour. If there are any darker edges to the sponges, remove them carefully using a fine grater.

Break the white chocolate into smaller pieces and add to a large bowl. Heat the double cream until it starts to gently bubble. Remove from the heat and pour over the white chocolate pieces. Allow it to stand for a minute or so then stir continuously until all the chocolate has melted. Cool this mixture in the fridge for at least an hour. In the meantime, put a few good tablespoons of quality raspberry jam into a pan and add a couple of drops of rose essence – not enough to overpower it though. Warm gently, stirring all the time. Once the white chocolate cream mixture has completely cooled, use an electric whisk to whip it until the cream has doubled in size and turned very light and fluffy.

To assemble, cut the cake into two halves through the middle. Place the bottom layer onto a plate and spread with the jam. Next, spread on about half of the cream, taking care not to go too close to the edges. Put the top layer of sponge on and, using a spatula, spread the rest of the cream around the edge of the cake and covering the top. Sprinkle the chopped pistachios across the top and press them around the sides of the cake. Decorate with whole fresh strawberries if desired.

Antony Worrall Thompson
SOMETHING FOR ELEVENSES

//

This is such an easy bar to make and ideal to eat anywhere, either at home or the office. Why not have a coffee morning in aid of BBC Children in Need? Everyone has to stop for Elevenses, even the great Pudsey Bear! And if you don't fancy hibiscus or pomegranate, both healthy juices, then you could substitute it with apple juice. They last for up to a week in a container. So ditch the 'processed' bars and bake some of these – you won't be disappointed.

MAKES 9

325g of your favourite dried fruits (I like dried apples, apricots, pears and blueberries)
200g 'no nuts' muesli
½ tsp mixed spice
½ tsp cinnamon
¼ tsp five spice powder
75ml hibiscus or pomegranate juice
2 tbsp runny honey
65g wholemeal flour
Spray of oil

METHOD

Pulse the dried fruit in a food-processor until well chopped but not puréed. Combine the fruit with the muesli and spices.

Meanwhile heat the juice and honey in a large saucepan then stir in the flour followed by the muesli mixture. Stir well to combine.

Preheat the oven to 200°C (gas mark 6).

Line a 25cm square or rectangular shallow baking dish with parchment paper and lightly spray with oil. Tip the mixture into the dish and smooth over the contents.

Bake in the oven for 25 minutes, checking from time to time to make sure they are not getting too brown; if they are, reduce the oven temperature to 180°C (gas mark 4).

Allow to cool, turn out, then peel back the paper and cut into squares or rectangles, depending on the shape of your tray. Store in an airtight container for up to one week.

Antony is one of Britain's best-loved chefs. He became a staple on our TV screens and has written numerous bestselling books, including Real Family Food, Fast Family Food and The Essential Low Fat Cookbook.

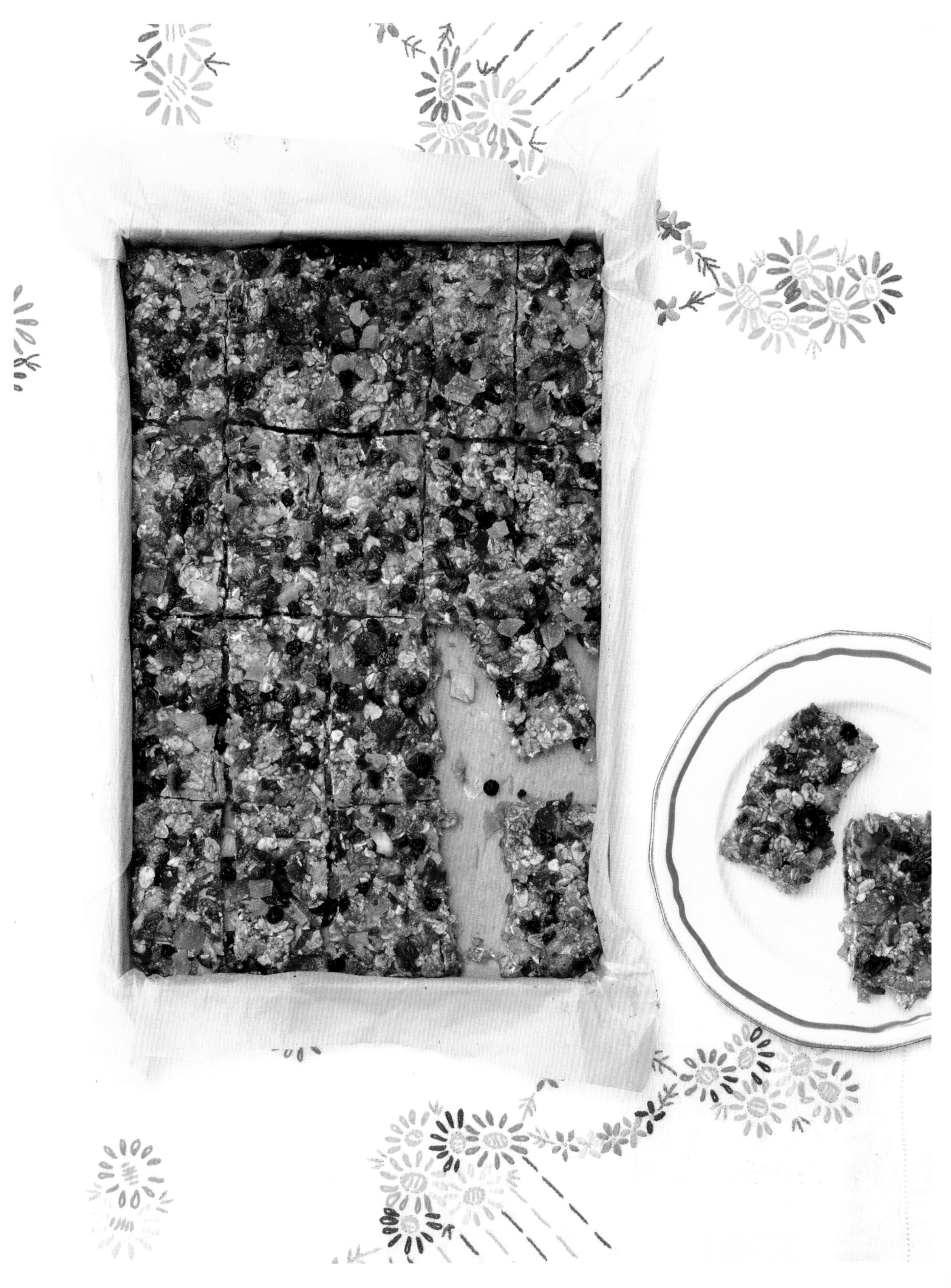

Beryl Stewart
RASPBERRY TIRAMISU

//

SERVES 6

250g mascarpone cheese
300ml of good quality readymade custard
12 boudoir fingers
Glass of dry white wine or elderflower cordial
340g raspberries (fresh or frozen)
Grated dark chocolate or cocoa powder, to sprinkle

METHOD

Beat the mascarpone and custard together.

Put the raspberries in the base of a nice dish. Dip the boudoir fingers in the wine or cordial. Press these on top of the raspberries to release a little juice from the fruit. Cover with the mascarpone mixture and smooth the top. Cover liberally with grated chocolate or cocoa powder.

Chill and serve.

Beryl Stewart, Upton
"I am a retired civil servant (I was one of the hard-working ones!). I used to buy plastic freezer bags from Lakeland when they had just the one place in the Lakes; I used to order them with a friend by mail order (oh those were the days!). I love Lakeland because they have quirky things, like moulds to make chocolate spoons. It is the only shop I love that my husband loves too so he gives me plenty of time to browse (he usually spends more than I do!)."

Catherine Penman
TRIPLE CHOCOLATE, CHERRY & WALNUT MUFFINS

//

This recipe is very simple but has a luxurious combination of flavours. I like to eat one after it has been kept in the fridge so that the chocolate chips have a bite to them.

SERVES 4

100g plain chocolate chips
100g white chocolate chips
200g glacé cherries, halved
55g walnuts, chopped
170g soft light brown sugar
110g self-raising wholewheat flour
225g self-raising white flour
2 tsp baking powder
1 tbsp cocoa
55g butter, melted
1 large egg beaten with 235ml milk

You will need:
1 x 12-hole muffin tin lined with
Lakeland muffin cases

METHOD

Put all the dry ingredients into a bowl then add the melted butter and egg and milk mixture.

Stir with a metal spoon until the mixture is well combined then spoon into the muffin cases.

Bake at 200°C for approximately 15-20 minutes.

Leave to cool on a wire rack.

Catherine Penman, Sunderland
"It's hard to pick just one thing that I love about Lakeland, there are so many! The staff are without a doubt first class. I would go so far as to say they are the best customer service people I have ever dealt with."

Edd Kimber
RED VELVET CAKE

//

Red velvet is such a great cake for a party. It has a beautiful white exterior but when you cut into the cake you get a beautiful red cake, so impressive! It's not quite a chocolate cake but the cocoa in the recipe gives a rich depth of flavour and it pairs beautifully with the cream cheese frosting, perfect for any occasion.

SERVES 12-16

For the cake:
225g unsalted butter, room temperature
350g plain flour, plus some for dusting
3 tbsp boiling water
2 tsp red paste food colouring
40g cocoa powder
250ml buttermilk
1 tsp baking soda
¼ tsp salt
350g caster sugar
3 large eggs, lightly beaten
1 tsp vanilla extract
1 tbsp white or cider vinegar

For the cream cheese frosting:
250g unsalted butter, room temperature
500g icing sugar
400g full fat cream cheese
1 tsp vanilla extract

After winning the BBC2 series The Great British Bake Off in 2010, Edd's life has been a rollercoaster journey in food. He has written two cookbooks, The Boy Who Bakes and Say It With Cake.

METHOD

Preheat the oven to 180°C (fan 160°C) and grease three 20cm/8-inch round cake tins and line with parchment, greasing the parchment too. Dust the tins with a little extra flour, tapping out any excess.

In a small bowl, mix together the boiling water, food colouring, cocoa powder and buttermilk, mixing until fully combined then set aside. Sift the flour, baking soda and salt into a medium bowl. Using an electric mixer, fitted with the paddle attachment, beat the butter and sugar until light and fluffy, about five minutes.

Beat in the eggs a little at a time, beating until fully combined before adding more. Once all of the egg has been added, mix in the vanilla extract and then in three additions beat in the flour mixture, alternating with the buttermilk (starting and finishing with the flour). To finish stir in the vinegar.

Divide the mixture between the prepared tins and bake in the preheated oven for 25-30 minutes or until a skewer inserted into the middle of the cakes come out clean. Allow to cool in the tins for about 10 minutes before turning out onto wire racks to cool completely.

To make the frosting place the butter into the bowl of an electric mixer, fitted with the paddle attachment, and beat for about three minutes or until light and creamy. Beat in the icing sugar, a little at a time, beating until you have a light and fluffy buttercream. Add the cream cheese and vanilla extract and beat until you have a smooth buttercream.

To assemble, place a layer of cake onto a serving plate or cake board and top with just under a third of the frosting, spreading into a smooth layer. Repeat with the second layer of cake and finish by placing the last layer of cake on top. Spread the remaining frosting across the top and sides of the cake and serve.

Frances Quinn
CHOCOLATE MEDAL BISCUITS

//

My chocolate coin medals are a tasty way of using up an assortment of chocolate coins, which although cheap in value are rich in taste. The combination of ginger biscuits and chocolates works brilliantly, but feel free to omit the ginger and use cinnamon or mixed spice if you prefer or simply flavour them with the vanilla extract. A variety of ribbons can be used to create different winning medals whatever the occasion or celebration.

MAKES APPROX. 30 BISCUITS

For the biscuits:
125g slightly salted butter, softened
125g light brown muscovado sugar
1 egg, lightly beaten
1 tsp vanilla extract
1 tsp ginger
250g plain flour, plus some for dusting

Decoration:
Packet of gold and silver coins
Ribbon or string

Frances Quinn is renowned for her creativity. A British baker and designer, she was the inimitable winner of The Great British Bake Off 2013. A star set to ignite and mix up the baking and design scene, in Britain and beyond.

METHOD

Preheat the oven to 180°C.

Cream together the butter and sugar, then gradually beat in the egg and vanilla extract. Sift and stir in the flour and ginger and mix to a fairly soft dough. Turn onto a lightly floured surface and knead gently. Cover or wrap the dough in clingfilm and chill for at least an hour or preferably overnight. When ready, roll the dough out on a lightly floured surface to around 0.2cm thick.

Take your chocolate coins and pick out circular cutters approx 1cm wider than the coins in diameter. Cut out your medal biscuits with your appropriate sized cutters or by cutting round a paper template.

Transfer the biscuits onto a baking tray lined with baking parchment and make a hole near the top of the medals with the tip of a paintbrush or skewer. Bake in the oven for approx 5-10 minutes, depending on the size of the medals until the biscuits edges turn golden in colour. Once out of the oven leave the biscuits on the baking tray to cool slightly.

While the biscuits are still a bit warm remove one half of the foil on your chocolate coins and press, chocolate side down on to their surface to adhere to the medal. The warmth from the biscuits should slightly melt the chocolate and once cooled stick and set both together. If the biscuits have cooled too much you can either place them back in the oven for a short blast of heat or equally melt a chocolate coin and use the melted chocolate to act as edible glue to stick the coins to the biscuits.

Leave the chocolate coins to set and then thread either lengths of ribbon or string through the holes at the top of your medals.

Jenny Tschiesche

CASHEW, APRICOT & GINGER SQUARES

//

SERVES 4

230g cashews (100g of which should be salted)
200g dried (ideally unsulphured) apricots
4 cubes crystallised ginger
1½ tsp warm filtered water

For the icing:
3 tbsp coconut oil
1 tbsp honey
1 heaped tsp ground ginger

METHOD

Grind the nuts to a powder in a food processor.

Add all other ingredients and whizz to a dough.

Remove and place into a square baking tray lined with greaseproof paper.

Bake for 20 minutes at 160°C. Leave to cool.

Once cooled put the icing ingredients together in a saucepan and melt for about one minute over a medium heat. Take off the heat and whisk rapidly until you get a caramel-like consistency. Spread this on the cooled base.

Leave in the fridge to cool then chop into squares once the icing has set.

Jenny Tschiesche is a Lakeland customer from Slough.

June Wright
MRS MORRIS'S CHRISTMAS PUDDING

//

SERVES 4

110g plain flour
½ tsp salt
1 tsp salt
1 tsp mixed spice
1 tsp cinnamon
½ tsp ground nutmeg
225g shredded suet (can be vegetarian suet)
280g fresh white breadcrumbs
Juice and grated rind of 1 lemon and 1 orange
225g Demerara sugar
110g carrots, grated
110g cooking apple, grated
900g mixed dried fruit
55g flaked almonds
2 tbsp black treacle
4 eggs, lightly whisked
50ml Cointreau or brandy (I double up and use both!)
100ml Guinness or stout (optional)

METHOD

Sieve flour, salt and spices together into a large mixing bowl. Add all the dry ingredients and mix thoroughly.

Melt treacle in a pan, stir in the lemon and orange juice, Cointreau and/or brandy and lightly whisked eggs. Pour the liquid into the pudding mixture and stir thoroughly. If the mixture is still a little dry stir in the Guinness or stout.

Cover the basin with a cloth and leave until the next day,

Butter two 1.1 litre basins and spoon in the pudding mixture. Cover with a double layer of buttered greaseproof paper and then a double layer of foil or a saucer and cloth tied with string. Steam for 5-6 hours in pans of simmering water.

When cold recover the basins and store in a cool place.

On Christmas Day, steam for a further 2-3 hours.

If you want smaller puddings, cook for three hours initially then a further two on the day. They keep for up to a couple of years!

June Wright, Loughborough
"This recipe is one handed to my mother-in-law in the seventies by her then elderly neighbour, a wonderful old lady from the valleys of Wales. We have used it as a Christmas pudding for all family Christmases since."

Marlene Carpenter
CONDENSED MILK FRUIT CAKE

///

The mixture can be made into a large cake or smaller cakes and covered cellophane to make great little Christmas gifts. This recipe has been in our family for many years. It's great that there is no need for sugar or eggs. An Irish friend of mine said this cake was better than their traditional ones, and has always been a favourite!

SERVES 4

3 x 375g packet mixed fruit
395g tin condensed milk
312g plain flour
250g butter, chopped
250ml water
1 tbsp vinegar
2 tbsp sherry or brandy, plus some to finish
1 tsp bicarbonate of soda
1 tsp vanilla essence
1 tsp baking powder
½ tsp salt
½ ground cloves
Cherries and almonds, to garnish

Note: You could replace some of the fruit with raisins or apricots and add some nuts.

METHOD

Put the mixed fruit, butter, soda and water in a pan and bring to the boil. Allow to cool.

Add the condensed milk, vinegar, sherry or brandy and vanilla essence.

Sift the flour, baking powder, salt and ground cloves and gradually add to the fruit mixture.

Put into a greased paper lined tin, put a cherry in each corner and one in the centre and place almonds to make a flower effect.

Bake at 150°C for two hours.

Check with a skewer and adjust cooking time if necessary.

When cooked put on a rack and brush with sherry or brandy.

Marlene Carpenter, Moonta, South Australia
"What I love most about Lakeland is the service and quick delivery, even though I live in Australia. I look forward to the catalogues and browsing through – so much to see, and so different, which is a bonus!"

Pat Lee

MINI LEMON, MARMALADE & POPPY SEED LOAVES

//

SERVES 4

150g softened butter
150g caster sugar
2 large eggs
100g lemon marmalade, plus 1 tbsp to brush over the cakes
Juice and finely grated rind of 1 small lemon
Small squeeze of honey
100g self-raising flour
75g plain wholemeal flour
1 tsp baking powder
2 tsp poppy seeds
25g toasted flaked almonds

METHOD

Preheat the oven to 180°C and place loaf cases onto a baking tray.

Whisk the butter and sugar together in a bowl until light and fluffy.

Whisk the eggs in one at a time.

Gently whisk in the 100g of lemon marmalade and the grated lemon rind.

Sift in the self-raising flour and baking powder, then stir in the poppy seeds and wholemeal flour with a fork. Add to the butter mix.

Fold in the almonds and spoon the mix into cases (approximately 90g each).

Bake for 20-25 minutes until golden and cooked throughout.

Mix the remaining one tablespoon of marmalade with one teaspoon of the lemon juice and the small squeeze of runny honey and brush over the cakes while still warm

Put the kettle on, make a brew and sit down and enjoy your bake. Yummy!

Pat Lee, Portslade, Sussex
"I entered the competition because everyone I make these cakes for just loves them, including my daughter who is really fussy. I have been a customer with Lakeland for approximately 15 years, maybe longer. I love the customer services, products and the 'no quibble' returns – where else in the country would you get this service?"

Pat Stott
THE DUKE'S CHRISTMAS CAKE

//

This was given to me by an old lady who had worked in the kitchens of a local stately home. The cake was always made when a 'certain' duke joined them in the hunting season. It has served me well at weddings, christenings, anniversaries and of course Christmas for many years.

SERVES 4

450g plain flour
450g soft dark brown sugar
450g butter
680g currants, soaked in 5 tbsp brandy or
orange juice overnight
110g cherries
110g mixed peel
4 medium eggs
110g ground almonds
285ml stout or Guinness
1 level tsp bicarbonate of soda
Grated rind of 1 lemon
3 level tsp mixed spice

METHOD

Sieve the flour, almonds and spice together then rub in the butter. Add the fruit and lemon rind and mix well.

Warm the stout or Guinness and beat in the eggs, then add the bicarbonate of soda (it will froth up). Stir into the dry ingredients and stir really well until completely mixed together.

Put into a greased and lined 22cm/9-inch cake tin, wrapped in brown paper. Make a small dip in the top to ensure the surface is even for icing.

Bake at 140°C for 3–3.5 hours or until a skewer comes out clean.

Leave it in the tin until cool then wrap in greaseproof paper and foil until ready to be iced (optional). I like to spike it with brandy a few times while waiting.

**Pat Stott,
Northumberland**
"Every celebration deserves a good fruit cake and this one has served me well on many occasions. I have baked it for Christmases, birthdays, christenings and for my 25th wedding anniversary.
Hopefully I will bake it again for my golden wedding."

Patricia Woods
CELEBRATION GINGER CAKE

//

SERVES 4

170g margarine
340g treacle or golden syrup
110g soft brown sugar
4 tsp ground ginger
200ml milk
1 tsp bicarbonate of soda
340g self-raising flour
2 eggs

For the icing:
220g margarine
450g icing sugar

METHOD

Put the margarine, treacle/syrup, soft brown sugar and ground ginger into a bowl and heat in the microwave until it bubbles and the sugar is melted (approximately two minutes).

Warm up the milk in a microwave for about 30 seconds.

Stir in the bicarbonate of soda – it should dissolve or maybe froth up a bit.

Add the flour and the eggs.

Add the milky solution to your treacle mixture and stir or whisk quickly so all the flour lumps have dispersed.

Pour into a lined 20cm/8-inch square cake tin.

Place in a preheated oven at 180°C for 10-12 minutes.

Allow to cool.

For the icing, mix together the margarine and icing sugar.

The cake can be frozen and used at your convenience meaning you can make it well in advance of your party, making it so much easier for yourself.

It can be used as a cake or a warm pudding – it's easy to make and tastes great! Enjoy!

Patricia Woods, Surrey
"Next year (2015) I will be celebrating my 25th wedding anniversary and my 25th anniversary of being a Lakeland customer! What I love most about Lakeland is the quality of the products – I have never been disappointed with anything I have bought. I entered the competition because I thought this was a lovely way of Lakeland celebrating their anniversary and I thought my recipe was exactly the sort of cake that all Lakeland customers would enjoy."

Pauline Clements

LUSCIOUS LEMON BUNDT CAKE WITH PEACH SCHNAPPS GLAZE

///

SERVES 4

For the cake:
350g butter, softened, plus extra for greasing
350g caster sugar
4 large lemons – zest of all 4 plus juice of 2
6 free range eggs
3 tbsp baking powder
300g self-raising flour
50g cornflour

For the glaze:
100g caster sugar
Juice of 1 lemon
3 tbsp peach schnapps

Pauline Clements, Lichfield
"For me food is a central part of any family gathering or celebration (maybe it's my Scottish roots) and this recipe is the one that is always requested. There is something special about being able to provide sustenance for your nearest and dearest and that idea of 'giving' lends itself to my recipe being part of a cookbook that helps support a wonderful charity, while also celebrating 50 years of a company who provide products that help me look after my family."

METHOD

Preheat the oven to 160°C.

Grease a bundt tin well using melted butter and a pastry brush to get into all the details.

Cream the butter and sugar together in a bowl until pale and fluffy. Add the lemon zest and juice and mix, reserving some of the zest for decoration.

Slowly beat in the eggs, one at a time, until the mixture is well combined (you can add a little of the flour if the mixture begins to curdle).

Sift the baking powder, self-raising flour and cornflour into the bowl and fold into the cake mixture.

Pour all the batter into the tin. This should fill it to 2-3cm from the top of the tin. Give the tin a gentle bang on the kitchen surface to dislodge any air bubbles.

Bake for 40 minutes and then test with a cake tester or skewer and if the tester doesn't come out clean, continue to bake for 10 minute intervals until golden brown and cooked through.

Remove from the oven and set aside to cool in the tin for 10 minutes.

Place all the glaze ingredients into a saucepan and heat gently until all the sugar is dissolved.

While the cake is still in the tin, gently drizzle some of the warm glaze so that it soaks into the bundt. Leave for a few minutes.

Turn out onto a cooling rack and allow to cool completely.

Once cool drizzle the glaze over the bundt and shake a little icing sugar over the top. Add some lemon zest to decorate.

Pauline Dale
HOMEMADE CHILLI, TOMATO & FIG CHUTNEY

//

This is delicious served with cheese and crackers, or cold meats. Also great to give away as gifts.

MAKES ENOUGH FOR 2 JARS

500g red onions
500g tomatoes
175g dried figs
4 garlic cloves
1 large red chilli
2 tsp fresh grated ginger
1 tsp celery salt
1 tsp smoked paprika
2 cardamom pods
250g soft brown sugar
150ml red wine vinegar

METHOD

Sterilise and prepare two 90g (2lb) Lakeland jam jars.

Peel and finely slice the red onions and garlic and add to a large pan with the sugar and vinegar.

Roughly chop the tomatoes and figs and add to the pan.

Carefully deseed and finely chop the red chilli pepper and add to the pan along with grated ginger. Leave the seeds in the chilli if you like more heat.

Add the celery salt, paprika and cardamom pods, slightly crushed.

Give the ingredients a good stir.

Place a lid on the pan and simmer for one hour. After one hour, remove the lid and turn up the heat until the mixture begins to boil gently. After around 20-30 minutes the liquid will have reduced to a sticky jam-like consistency. Turn off the heat and allow the chutney to cool slightly.

While still warm, remove the cardamom pods and pour the chutney into the prepared jars.

Wait until the chutney is completely cool in the jars before adding the lids.

Pauline Dale, Manchester
"Lakeland always seem to be that one step ahead of anywhere else in terms of the products on offer. I mean, where else would you find a croquembouche kit on the high street? I came across the competition via the Lakeland Facebook page and thought it would be a fantastic opportunity to feature in one of their recipe books."

Pooja Patel
BERRY BAKEWELL SQUARES

//

SERVES 10-12

250g unsalted butter, plus some for greasing
200g golden caster sugar
1 tsp vanilla extract
3 large eggs
200g self-raising flour
50g ground almonds
¼ tsp salt
100g blueberries
100g raspberries
75g blackberries
Handful flaked almonds
1 tbsp icing sugar, to finish

METHOD

Butter and line a baking tray or small roasting tin, about 20cm x 30cm. Heat the oven to 180°C (fan 160°C).

Gently melt the butter in a large saucepan, cool for five minutes, add the sugar, vanilla and eggs then beat until smooth with a wooden spoon. Stir in the flour, ground almonds and salt.

Top the mix into the tin, then scatter the mixture of blueberries, blackberries and raspberries evenly on top – that way each square of cake will have a bite of fruit.

Sprinkle the flaked almonds over, then bake for 60-70 minutes, covering with foil after 40 minutes. Test with a skewer: the middle should just have a tiny hint of squidginess, which will firm up once the cake cools.

Cool in the tin for 20 minutes, then lift out onto a cooling rack. Once cold, dredge with icing sugar, then cut into squares.

Happy baking!

Pooja Patel is a Lakeland customer from Harrow.

Sheila Nicholas
TORTA DEL CIELO ('CAKE OF HEAVEN')

//

This cake is great with coffee for breakfast. It is wonderful with raspberries and a good vanilla ice cream for dessert. It freezes beautifully and due to its shallowness cuts well while still frozen, if you only need a slice or two. I don't usually dust with icing sugar until ready to serve. Garnish with flaked almonds if desired.

SERVES 12
225g butter
175g ground almonds
225g caster sugar
3 eggs, gently beaten
1 tsp almond essence
1 tsp vanilla essence
70g plain flour
Icing sugar, for dusting
Flaked almonds (optional)

You will need:
26cm/10-inch shallow round tin, greased
with parchment base lining

METHOD
Preheat the oven to 170°C.

Cream together the butter and sugar until light and fluffy.

Gently beat in the ground almonds, eggs and essences until well mixed.

Sift flour into the bowl to combine the ingredients.

Add the mix to the baking tin and place in the centre of the oven for about 40 minutes. Test with a skewer, which needs to come out clean.

Remove from the oven and allow to cool.

Add flaked almonds and dust with icing sugar to serve (optional).

Sheila Nicholas, Midhurst, Sussex
"Lakeland provides solutions to many baking and household queries. I have been a customer for as long as the Chichester branch has been open. I entered on a whim – saw the email, had a while to spare and wrote the recipe out."

Sir Terry Wogan
SIR TERRY'S LEMON DRIZZLE CAKE

//

Sir Terry Wogan is BBC Children in Need's Life President and has hosted the seven-hour live BBC Children in Need Appeal TV show since 1980. Sir Terry is a veteran TV and radio presenter who began his career at Radio Telefis Eirann in the 1960s. In 1967, Sir Terry began his long standing BBC partnership presenting "Late Night Extra" and in 1972 he took over "The Breakfast Show" on BBC Radio 2, where Wogan enjoyed unprecedented popularity, leaving to focus on a full-time TV career in 1984.

In 1982 Sir Terry's small screen career, which began on the BBC's "Blankety Blank", entered Saturday evening peak time with the BBC One chat show "Wogan". This popular piece of evening entertainment won him an army of fans and established Sir Terry Wogan as the country's top TV chat show host. The programme was aired three times a week for seven years and was followed by a weekly show on BBC One "Friday Night With Terry Wogan".

In 1993 Sir Terry returned to his old stomping ground at Radio 2, five mornings a week presenting "Wake Up To Wogan", once again enjoying the same kind of popularity that elected him the title "Outstanding Radio Personality of the Past 25 Years". He stepped down from his Radio 2 seat at the end of 2009 and now presents his new primetime Sunday show on Radio 2 "Weekend Wogan" which started in February 2010.

SERVES 8

For the cake:
5 eggs
300g caster sugar
140ml double cream
Butter, for greasing
Zest of 2 lemons (finely grated)
240g plain flour
2g baking powder
1 pinch of salt

For the glaze:
40g apricot jelly (heated in a saucepan)
30ml lemon juice
Zest of ½ lemon (finely grated)
165g icing sugar

METHOD

Preheat the oven to 170°C.

In a large bowl whisk together the eggs, sugar, cream and lemon zest.

Sieve together the flour and baking powder twice, add to the bowl followed by the salt. Whisk until smooth.

Grease your loaf tin with a little softened butter and line with greaseproof paper. Fill the tin with the mixture and bake in the preheated oven for 40 minutes, turning halfway.

To check if it's cooked insert a small knife blade into the middle of the cake, if it comes out clean it is done. Turn it out onto a baking rack and leave to cool.

To finish brush the cake all over with the hot apricot glaze.

In a small saucepan gently warm the lemon juice, zest and icing sugar to form the glaze. Brush the glaze over the cake and leave for a few minutes.

//

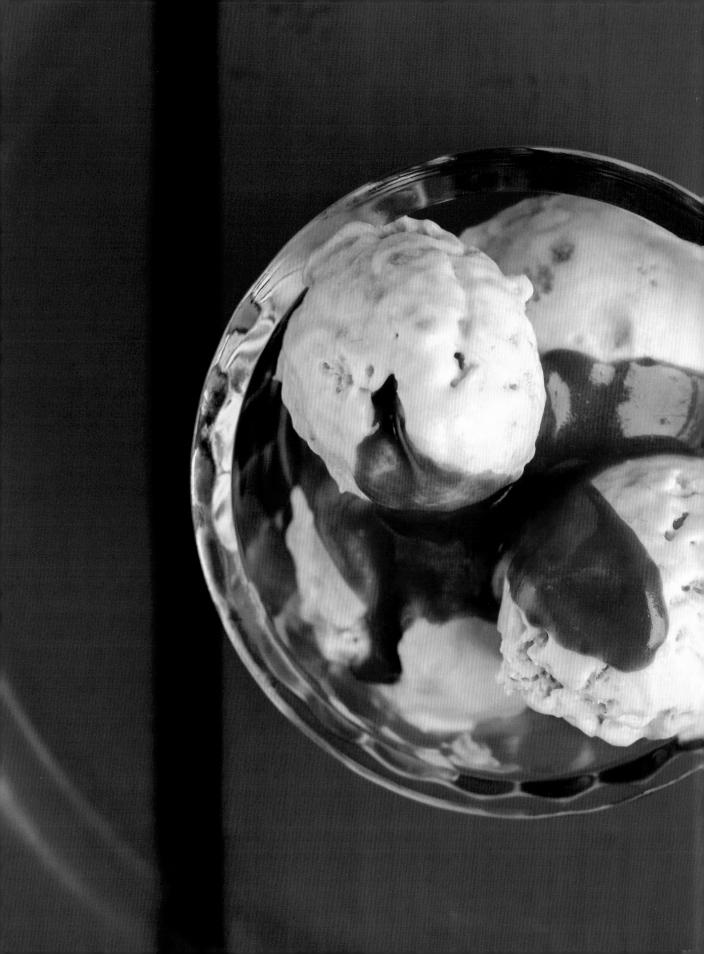

INDEX OF RECIPES

GINGER

Cashew, apricot & ginger squares 156
Celebration ginger cake 166
Pepper & lime ginger cakes 140

HAM

Celebration quiche 98
Chicken stuffed with goats' cheese, serrano ham & tomato 76

ICE CREAM

Banoffee ice cream 116

LAMB

Giouvetski 74

LEMON

Lemon meringue roulade 110
Luscious lemon bundt cake with peach schnapps glaze 168
Mini lemon, marmalade & poppy seed loaves 162
Sir Terry's lemon drizzle cake 176

LIME

Pepper & lime ginger cakes 140

MACKEREL

Smackers (homemade smoked mackerel pâté) 46

MOUSSE

White chocolate & tangerine mousse 102

MUSHROOMS

Maaaarvellous mushrooms 54
Stuffed mushrooms with garlic and cheese 36

NUTS

Cashew, apricot & ginger squares 156
Double chocolate nutty roulade 112
Nancy's almond delights 126

Raspberry, hazelnut & framboise chocolate brownies 138
Rose & pistachio cake with white chocolate ganache 144
Triple chocolate, cherry & walnut muffins 150
White chocolate & pistachio sponge blondies 128

ORANGE

Tomato & sherry soup 56
White chocolate & tangerine mousse 102

PASTA

Giouvetski 74
Italian fusilli sausage 'ragu' 60
King prawn linguine with chilli, garlic & asparagus 78

PÂTÉ

Smackers (homemade smoked mackerel pâté) 46

PEAR

Pear tarte tatin 104

PHEASANT

Faisan Archiduc (pheasant stuffed with truffle and foie gras) 82
Mother's pheasant with port, celery & cream 66

PIE

Chicken & potato pie 92
Smoked fish pie 68

POTATO

Chicken & potato pie 92
Rich venison casserole with mustard mash 62
Salmon, dill & new potato tart 50
Smoked fish pie 68
Triple-cooked chips 80

PRAWN

King prawn linguine with chilli, garlic & asparagus 78

QUICHE

Celebration quiche 98

RASPBERRY

Raspberry, hazelnut & framboise chocolate brownies 138
Raspberry tiramisu 148

RISOTTO

Remoska baked squash & stilton risotto 94

SALMON

Salmon, dill & new potato tart 50

SAUSAGE

Italian fusilli sausage 'ragu' 60
Sausage plait 86

SCALLOPS

Scallop gratin 42

SOUP

Tomato & sherry soup 56

TART

Apple tart 'Maman Blanc' 132
Pear tarte tatin 104
Salmon, dill & new potato tart 50

TOMATO

Chicken stuffed with goats' cheese, serrano ham & tomato 76
Homemade chilli, tomato & fig chutney 170
Italian fusilli sausage 'ragu' 60
Madras fish curry of snapper, tomato & tamarind 90
Tomato & sherry soup 56

VENISON

Rich venison casserole with mustard mash 62
Roasted rack of venison with spiced red cabbage 96

CONTRIBUTORS / CREDITS:

Sir Terry Wogan, Brian Turner, Frances Quinn, Jo Wheatley

The Hairy Bikers, Salmon, Dill & New Potato Tart

Copyright © Byte Brook Limited and Sharp Letter Limited, 2011.
Photography by Cristian Barnett. Extracted from The Hairy Bikers™ Perfect Pies by Si King and Dave Myers
Published by Weidenfeld & Nicolson
www.hairybikers.com

Ainsley Harriott, Italian Fusilli Sausage 'Ragu'

From Ainsley's Friends and Family Cookbook by Ainsley Harriott. Published by Ebury
Reprinted by permission of The Random House Group Limited. Photography Juliet Piddington

Heston Blumenthal, Triple-Cooked Chips

Image © Angela Moore. Taken from Heston Blumenthal at Home by Heston Blumenthal, published by Bloomsbury.

Michel Roux Jr, Faisan Archiduc

The French Kitchen, Michel Roux Jr, The Orion Publishing Group, London © Michel Roux Jr 2013.
Photography by Cristian Barnett

Paul Hollywood, Sausage Plait

Image © Peter Cassidy. Adapted from Paul Hollywood's Pies & Puds by Paul Hollywood, published by Bloomsbury.

Rick Stein, Madras Fish Curry of Snapper, Tomato & Tamarind

Extracted from Rick Stein's India by Rick Stein (Ebury Press, £25)

Rosemary Shrager, Chicken & Potato Pie

Rosemary Shrager's Bakes Cakes & Puddings published by Hamlyn
© photography Christian Barnett

Tom Kitchin, Roasted Rack of Venison with Spiced Red Cabbage

Kitchin Suppers by Tom Kitchin is published by Quadrille, priced £20. Photography © 2012 Laura Edwards.

Eric Lanlard, Pear Tarte Tatin

Taken from Home Bake by Eric Lanlard published by Mitchell Beazley
© photography Craig Robertson

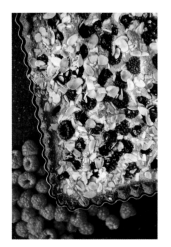

CONTRIBUTORS / CREDITS (CONTINUED):

Gregg Wallace, Cherry & Chocolate Cake
Photograph of Gregg © Charlotte Knee
Photograph of cake © Hilary Moore

James Martin, Ice Box Cake
Extracted from Fast Cooking by James Martin (Quadrille, £20)
Text © 2013 James Martin
Photograph © 2013 Tara Fisher

John Whaite, Chocolate Berry Frasier Cake
Photography © Matt Russell

Lorraine Pascale, White Chocolate & Pistachio Sponge Blondies
Extracted from A Lighter Way to Bake by Lorraine Pascale
Text © 2013 Lorraine Pascale
Photography © 2013 Myles New

Mary Berry, Large All-in-one Victoria Sandwich
Mary Berry's Baking Bible by Mary Berry (BBC Books, hardback £25)
Photography © Dan Jones

Raymond Blanc, Apple Tart 'Maman Blanc'
For more recipes by Raymond Blanc, please visit www.raymondblanc.com/recipes
Recipe from Kitchen Secrets by Raymond Blanc, published by Bloomsbury.
Photography © Jean Cazals 2011
Picture of Raymond © Paul Wilkinson 2014

Antony Worrall Thompson, Something for Elevenses
The Essential Low Fat Cookbook by Antony Worrall Thompson with Juliette Kellow BSc RD (Kyle Books, £20) with photography by Georgia Glynn Smith
Picture of Antony © Nick Ayliffe

Edd Kimber, Red Velvet Cake
Adapted from 'The Boy Who Bakes' (Kyle Books 2011)

Edited by:
Adam Kay, Martin Edwards, Chris Brierley, Paul Orton

Design by:
Richard Abbey

Photography by:
© Jodi Hinds Photography
www.jodihinds.com
Additional photographs supplied by Lakeland

First published in 2014 on behalf of:
Lakeland – www.lakeland.co.uk
Alexandra Buildings, Windermere, Cumbria, LA23 1BQ
Tel: 01539 488100

Published by:
RMC Books – www.rmcbooks.co.uk
5 Broadfield Court, Sheffield, S8 0XF
Tel: 0114 250 6300